The Free Mama

How to Work From Home, Control Your Schedule, and Make More Money

By Lauren Golden

THE FREE MAMA

P.O. Box 6296
Katy, TX 77491

Publisher: Elite Online Publishing
63 East 11400 South Suite #230
Sandy, UT 84070
www.EliteOnlinePublishing.com

ISBN: **978-1513626406**

Exclusive Bonus Chapter!

Would you like to read an unpublished chapter from *The Free Mama?*

I hope you enjoy reading *The Free Mama*! If you want even more, you can now sign up to get an exclusive, unpublished bonus chapter.

Have you ever finished a book or movie and totally wanted more? I know I have, and maybe that's why I wrote this additional chapter.

This Chapter is not published and is only available to readers on my e-mail list.

Just visit www.thefreemama.com/bookbonus to download this exclusive chapter from *The Free Mama*!

ACKNOWLEDGMENTS

To my parents: I don't know how much was nature and how much was nurture (and I suppose you'd be responsible for both!), but thank you for raising such a feisty, independent daughter. I have you to thank for always having the courage to go after what I want.

To my family: You are my everything. Justin, thank goodness we are both Dreamers or we may have never met and created this crazy life together. I love you. Daphne, Henry, and Audrey . . . I feel conflicted every day with wanting to freeze time and hold on to each precious moment of your childhood, and yet I cannot wait to witness the amazing people each of you will become.

To Liz and Kristi: Thank you for helping me fly.

To Abbi and Karin: Thank you for helping me put my thoughts into words!

And to all my Free Mamas, thank you for making our community what it is. You have touched my life much more than I have yours. Forever grateful.

Table of Contents

FOREWORD

When I was eight years old, I sold stolen beer to old men and made a fortune. And this was where my entrepreneurial journey began.

It got much more legitimate (and legal), of course. So let me back things up for a minute and tell you the whole story.

Even as a little girl, I wanted some money of my own and to buy things all by myself. So although I didn't know that's what I was doing, I started a business one summer.

Our house in Overland Park, Kansas, sat at the end of a cul-de-sac and backed up to the Deer Creek Golf Course—so close, in fact, that I'd fill entire grocery sacks with the golf balls I fished out of the bottom of our pool. If a golfer was unlucky enough to hit a stray shot into our yard while I was there, I'd try to sell it back to them. I'd hop off the trampoline and start making deals.

My friends and I would fill grocery sacks with golf balls, load them onto my little red wagon, wheel it down the driveway, and head down a small hill to a wrought-iron fence where we'd set up shop.

At eight, I thought for sure that the neon golf balls would be my top sellers, but it turned out nobody wanted those; they wanted the bright-white ones.

Supply and demand. I started charging *more* for clean white golf balls.

Still, golf balls overall were a slow mover. We tried lemonade, but that was a bust as well. Next up: soda.

My family kept soda in a spare fridge in my parents' built-in bar, so we raided the fridge, headed down the hill to the wrought-iron fence, and sold the cans for a dollar a pop. It was a great gig, but one day we ran out of product.

No problem. We moved on to Bud Light. We loaded a cooler of ice onto the wagon, the Bud Light into the cooler, and headed back down the hill to sell beer through a fence. We even had an upsell: Want to add on a golf ball with that Bud Light?

By the time the authorities—my parents—found out, I had made more than $500 in a couple months' time.

While I'm sure I got in some trouble for stealing from the fridge, what I remember most is that my dad, who's a business owner himself, turned it into a learning opportunity.

He taught me I needed to reimburse my distributor (him) and that inventory is not free. We arranged a fair wholesale price for the soda and beer I had taken.

Next, we tackled the importance of managing your finances as a business owner. He took me to the bank to open my first checking and savings accounts, with him as cosigner, and he made me put 25 percent of my earnings into the savings account. Then I was allowed to do what I wanted with the remainder.

Rather than invest it back in the business (now that my parents were in on it, the beer was out), I had my dad drive me to Toys"R"Us, where I bought a snow-cone machine. That one wasn't for business; it was all for me.

Supply and demand, inventory, finances, and the sweet reward of a smart business idea.

I was hooked.

INTRODUCTION

One week after my miscarriage, I walked into my boss's office and quit my job.

It wasn't a rash decision made in the middle of grief. Really, it was the opposite. Tragedy had given me clarity.

I had two babies and a job, and I was making plans to work from home—eventually. In a year or so. If everything went the way I planned.

The thing about a year, I've learned, is that it's close enough it makes you feel like it will happen and far enough it doesn't cause heart palpitations.

I was taking my time trying to figure out a side gig that could replace my income and thought I had plenty of it. My job was fine, even if not totally fulfilling. My husband, Justin, was getting his own business off the ground, making me the breadwinner and benefits holder, so I'd laid out a timeline and a plan that was solid but not urgent. It felt safe.

It was the middle of July—just a few months into my yearlong plan—when I unexpectedly found out I was pregnant.

I remember taking the pregnancy test at my parents' house, where I was dropping off the kids so Justin and I could take a quick anniversary weekend getaway in Branson, Missouri. I was anxiously bouncing around the bathroom trying to keep quiet while I waited, and yet I couldn't help but smile when I saw the pink plus sign.

Now, if you know me, you know that being quiet isn't my strong suit. Which is why I was so proud of myself for keeping the news a secret from my entire family while I said my goodbyes before heading out to pick my husband up from work and hit the road. And then I even managed to keep it a secret from him the entire three-hour drive.

He caught on when we went out to dinner and I turned down a margarita (my favorite). I had told him to drink up because he was set with a designated driver for another nine months, and he laughed.

"Are you kidding?" he asked, finally catching on.

Then he shuffled between excitement and panic throughout dinner before settling on genuine happiness. It didn't take us long to start throwing out baby-name ideas. Our new yearlong plan started to take shape, and my maternity leave was the perfect exit strategy.

When I called to make my first doctor's appointment, I was incredibly irritated to find out they no longer accepted our insurance. Maybe it was the hormones, but the last thing I wanted was to start over with someone new for my third child.

For some reason, Justin had let his staff know he wouldn't be coming in that morning so he could be with me at that appointment. He had gone to maybe three others between our daughter and son, but he was at this one—what was supposed to be a routine twelve-week checkup.

Within a few minutes of meeting me, the new doctor had to give me the worst news of my life. At the time, I wasn't sure if I felt worse for her or me.

I'm pretty sure time stopped.

I remember being so thankful I didn't have to sit in the cold room by myself. Or walk over from her office to the main hospital for a confirmation ultrasound. It was dark in the room as I waited—feeling angry and hysterical—to have someone tell me what I already knew. My husband drove us home. When I got there, I laid down on the couch, alone, and felt sorry for myself. A coworker brought home my stuff from work.

I had to decide whether to let the baby pass naturally or to have a procedure done, an impossible choice. I decided to have the procedure because I felt like I wouldn't be able to start the healing process until it was "over"; at seven o'clock that night, my husband called the doctor for me to let her know I would go in for the D&C the next morning, a Saturday.

My three-year-old cuddled with me in bed. She cried because I cried and asked if she could touch my tummy and say goodbye to the baby. She told the baby she loved him. More tears.

I didn't sleep that night, scared for the surgery and nervous about something going wrong. The next morning, I was surrounded by women: my doctor, the nurses, the anesthesiologist. All of them women. Several grabbed my hand as if it to say they'd been there; it would be okay. It was overwhelming.

I gave my baby a gender and a name, which made it easier for me to grieve. My husband and I understood that everyone grieves in their own way, and because that kind of connection would make the loss more difficult for him, I kept it all between me and my baby.

I remember going back to my parents' house—the same place where I had taken the pregnancy test—after the surgery so I could rest in a quiet, toddler-free house. One of the strangest things I remember is how energetic I felt; my extreme morning sickness had vanished with the surgery and made me feel guilty that I physically felt better. I sat in the dark in the guest-room bed supported by a mountain of pillows and composed an email to my coworkers, then shared the email on Facebook.

Like my pregnancy, my miscarriage became incredibly public. I hadn't done so intentionally, but when you're as sick as I am during pregnancy—constantly running to the bathroom to throw up—it's pretty hard to keep it hidden for long. Just days before my doctor appointment, I had put our pregnancy out there on social media.

I shared news of the miscarriage not for my benefit but to help prevent an awkward foot-in-mouth moment for everyone in my life.

What Are You Waiting For?

I don't know who or what it was, but in my grief I kept hearing a voice in my head.

"What's your plan now?" it asked. "What's your new plan?"

I kept feeling the sense that I could plan and plan and plan, but I wasn't in control of it all.

We hadn't planned the pregnancy any more than we had the miscarriage.

The nagging voice led me to ask myself the question I had been avoiding: *What am I really waiting for*?

My long timeline had felt safe. A year had felt so far away. But what, really, had I been waiting for? There's no such thing as the perfect time or the perfect circumstance.

If I didn't do it now, when would I? It may sound crazy, but that miscarriage gave me the push I needed to start living my life the way I actually wanted to be living it. No more planning or excuses.

So I walked into work one week after the news and quit my job. Technically, I stayed on by request to help out through the remainder of 2015. Then, when the New Year came, 2016 was truly a new year.

At the time of my miscarriage, I had kinda wanted to punch people when they'd tell me that everything happened for a reason. Looking back, though, I now know that baby gave me a huge gift in life.

While I like to think I would have followed through with my plan to leave my job and build a business from home, I'm not positive I wouldn't have kept making excuses and stalling. It's called a comfort zone for a reason: it's comfy.

Yet that tragic and all-too-common experience sent me on a very different trajectory in my life. It's sometimes hard to believe it was only a couple of years ago I felt trapped by the nine-to-five and guilty for not showing up as the Mama I wanted to be. But life changes quickly when we embrace change.

I hope it doesn't take a tragedy for you to find your way. I'm here to help in any way I can, and this book will give you a load of information to noodle on—both motivational and practical.

I hope you'll join me in the Free Mama Movement, but only you can decide whether you want to do the work and get uncomfortable, and only you know what's best for your family.

My biggest message is one of choice. Life is full of choices. You chose when you say yes and when you say no.

You chose the company you keep. You chose what you have for breakfast.

There's only one choice I want all mothers to know that you should never, *ever* have to make: you don't have to choose between your family and financial stability.

You—and you alone—get to decide how you live your life, Mama. If you are feeling guilty, stuck, unfulfilled, or any other icky feeling right now, I'm going to show you how to create your own opportunity so that you can live a totally awesome, guilt-free life.

Section 1

The Truth about Having It All

CHAPTER 1

How a Classic Kid's Game Ruined Everything

Do you remember the MASH game? Mansion, apartment, shack, house! We took this fortune-teller game *very* seriously in my childhood.

In case you didn't grow up in the nineties, let me explain the rules. You'd write "MASH" across the top of a page, the names of prospective husbands and careers along the right side, numbers along the bottom to represent the number of children you'd have, and maybe four types of cars and potential cities to call home on the left side of the paper.

You'd have some swirling-pen method to determine your magic number, and the game began as you eliminated all options until your future revealed itself . . . mansion! . . . JTT (yesss!) . . . and so on.

When we played, we knew exactly what combinations we wanted—our dream MASH scenarios.

And you wanna know the crazy thing? A lot of us never outgrew that fantasy. We realized we weren't going to become the princess who married Prince Charming (Meghan Markle being the most recent exception), but we figured out we probably didn't need a mansion to be happy. Can you imagine *cleaning* a house that big anyway?

But the message still distorted our expectations somehow when it came to the idea of "having it all." Because, for some reason, a lot of Mamas still think "have it all" means picture-perfect—your ideal MASH scramble. Beautiful, smart, perfect children who never misbehave. Husbands with loaded wallets and faces like Brad Pitt who dad like Danny Tanner. Shiny new cars with big red bows on them, just like the commercials at Christmastime. Large, pristine houses.

If that's the life you really want, then I've got your back. Heck, go after it with everything you've got. And hire a maid.

But if not? Then don't! Stop trying to keep up with Kardashians and cozy up to this idea: having it all is a *state of mind*, not of net worth.

That's right—the *all* you've been trying to have has nothing to do with actual things. Not that things are bad. I love things! But not at the expense of feeling 100 percent at peace with my decisions and actions.

For me, having it all means feeling peacefully fulfilled. I'm living without regrets from sacrifice. I'm making choices and taking action on those choices and going after what I want in life, fully showing up as the person I want to be to my family and friends, and not doing things simply because the world thinks I should.

This book is about not having to choose between family and finances, which for many of the hundreds of Mamas I've had the pleasure of working with, can become the biggest source of regret and guilt. You *can* have both. You can be home with your family and also have a career. And you can be good at both. You can even be great!

For most of you, the have-it-all lifestyle will probably be about the simple things that too often seem out of reach: To be able to take your family on a vacation twice a year. Or to be there when your kiddo is sick without feeling like you're disappointing someone else. To be able to head to a friend's wedding out of state and not worry about the money, or whether you can take time off, or feel like you should spend that time with your kids instead because you haven't seen them enough.

That last one—ugh. That's me, Mama. I missed one of my best friend's bachelorette parties because I couldn't afford to go.

My friend Mindy stayed on the West Coast after we graduated from the University of San Diego while I tried to figure out how to be an adult in New York and Arizona before moving back to my hometown of Kansas City. The hard part about going to school far away from home is that a lot of your best friends wind up living far away too.

We stay in touch, often in the form of leaving each other lengthy assessments of the latest *Bachelor* episode via voicemail, and Mindy even came to my wedding . . . in Kansas. A true friend. But when I got the notice about her wedding announcement, I had never even met her fiancé, for which I felt terrible.

Her maid of honor planned a three-day weekend cruise, which really doesn't wind up being much more expensive than a hotel room plus food. Except for me and one other college pal, Brittany, who had the legitimate excuse of just having had a baby, all of her close girlfriends were able to go.

I kept looking at the travel expenses and then the credit card balance, and I couldn't make the numbers work without having a panic attack. I felt helpless. I felt crappy. It's not like I was asking for my own private yacht! I just wanted to be there for this moment. I wanted to be a good friend for my good friend.

The guilt I felt then and the regret I feel now is still worse than missing the event (and for the record, we did find a way to make it to the wedding). I felt like I had no choice and no control over any part of my life, no control over how much money I made or how much time off I had. I felt like I didn't get to make my own decisions.

That is *not* what I wanted my life to look like. I didn't want to be helpless and collecting regrets.

Having It All versus Doing It All

I'm gonna shoot straight with you, Mama. You've been duped. Somewhere around the invention of the internet, women were sold a *ginormous* lie.

We were led to believe—or somehow convinced ourselves—that our worth comes from our ability to *do* it all.

It gets worse.

Doing it all isn't even enough! We must do everything well, at all times, with a smile on our face.

Here's the first major lesson of this book (please have your highlighter handy): *having* it all is totally different from *doing* it all.

Doing it all is when you feel like you have to work eighty hours a week plus scrub the house, cook all the meals from scratch using locally sourced organic ingredients, volunteer at school and at the soup kitchen, make homemade snacks and homemade teacher gifts, and have all the laundry washed, ironed, folded and put away before gliding into the bedroom looking as sexy as Beyoncé.

Holy wow. Who even *does* that? Oh, wait—Pinterest does that! Or at least it leads us to believe that this type of superhuman really exists.

Step away from Pinterest for a minute, Mama. It's not real life. Neither are Instagram, Facebook, or any other app on your phone where people post about their "lives."

Think about it. Nobody is doing ALL of those things. You're scrolling through a bunch of different people and a bunch of different profiles and creating impossibly unrealistic expectations of yourself *for no reason at all.*

Sure, one person is the Martha Stewart of preschool arts and crafts. Another is good at birthday cakes. A third is good at home décor. A fourth is a pro at contouring. But you don't really want to have to wear makeup every day, do you? A fifth travels around in a souped-up RV. A sixth documents her CrossFit obsession. Have you seen her postbaby figure? Not fair. A seventh does meal prep for the week. An eighth makes nontoxic laundry detergent and household cleaners. A ninth cans her own fruits and vegetables. A tenth has a mommy blog with tens of thousands of followers.

Have I made my point yet? That is *not* one person.

No one is good at everything. So why are you killing yourself trying to be?

Exhaustion is not a badge of honor, my friend. It's not the default setting. Unless you have a newborn keeping you up all night, you should not be exhausted all the time. Are most moms tired? Sure. Children are exhausting. *You don't have to be.*

Did you hear that?

You don't have to be exhausted. Which means you are *choosing* to be exhausted.

I hereby give you permission to stop doing All. Those. Things. In fact, if you'd like to live a have-it-all lifestyle or improve your current situation, I insist on it.

It's within your power, Mama. You can do it.

Which brings me to my second highlighter moment. There's a famous quote I recite to myself every single day.

"Whether you think you can or think you cannot, you're right."

Write that Henry Ford quote down in red lipstick on your bathroom mirror and make it your new mantra.

If you think you can make money from home and be present for your kids and control your schedule—you're right. If you think you can't—you're right.

I've got another one for you while the lipstick is out: "Happiness is a choice."

I'm going to repeat that in a louder voice in case you didn't hear me the first time: "HAPPINESS IS A CHOICE."

Remember how I told you that having it all was a state of mind? So is happiness! There are a lot of people who play the victim and don't take responsibility for their lives, their situations, or their choices. It's a lot easier to point fingers than to accept blame.

So many people expect things or people to make them happy. They tell themselves they'll be able to do something great when they get rid of debt, or they'll pursue their own interests when the kids are older.

Tough love, Mama. These are excuses. It's up to you, and only you, to chase after what you want. And you'll probably get to your goals faster if you choose to be happy and grateful for everything in your life starting *now*. Whether you think you can or think you cannot, you're right.

You Do You

Now that you're in the right frame of mind, all happy and victimless, I want you to understand that the have-it-all lifestyle is not one-size-fits-all. Maybe you don't want any of the things I mentioned or not in the way I described them. That's totally cool!

It's all about what you want for yourself and your family—and for living your life with intention and without regret.

You can be a material girl if you want. But do it for the right reasons; make sure your choice is based on your needs and wants, not on someone else's standards or opinions. And certainly not because you're trying to keep up with anyone you saw on the internet.

As I write this book, I still have so many things I want to do. My list is different than yours, and it's constantly evolving. You're never going to "arrive" if you define having it all with stuff.

My life is far from perfect. Not even close. We still have debt from a failed business that bothers us and things that stress us out. Stains on our couch. A ten-year-old car. Bouts with head lice from summer camp. Not to mention you won't see me making cupcakes on Pinterest anytime soon.

Yet I have it all. I feel personally fulfilled to be able to work and build a business on my own terms, and blessed to be able to help other people do the same.

Over the last three years, I've worked with and interviewed so many Mamas enjoying freedom as business owners, which brings them even more happiness in other areas of their lives. They're more likely to take better care of themselves, and that allows them to give more of themselves to the people they love.

And they feel less guilt. I know, right? Can you imagine? Because of their choices and hard work, these Mamas are able to be there for their kids when they want to and when they're needed—which means they don't feel guilty about work time or adult time.

Are any their lives perfect? Hardly. And yet every single one of them has told me they feel like they have it all.

This book was created for anyone who wants to have it all—the career woman who craves flexibility, the stay-at-home mom who wants to contribute financially, and the women who know they are meant for more.

The have-it-all lifestyle is a mindset that comes with following your own path. My sweet spot is working with those moms who want to build home-based businesses to have more control of their time and income. But I believe that anyone can have it all and that anyone can choose happiness.

So let's do this, Mama!

CHAPTER 2

YOU ARE MEANT FOR MORE

I turned thirty-two this spring, and I'm still mad about something that happened half a lifetime ago. Have you been there? I know you have. So let me tell you about this soccer chick in my high school who royally ticked me off. And no offense to all the soccer chicks out there, but this one messed with the wrong girl.

I was sitting at a desk in the last row of AP English with my back against the wall—literally and figuratively. I was talking with three other girls. I know—a story that starts out with me talking. Go figure.

The other girls were all previously on the soccer team, and that year's tryouts were coming up. They were totally egging me on, telling me, "Lauren, you should totally join us at tryouts! Oh wait—*dance team*."

The thing was, I hadn't played soccer in three years because, instead, I had focused on the competitive dance team, which was a year-round activity at the all-girls high school I attended in Kansas City.

Activity. Dance wasn't called a sport because the state's athletic association didn't consider it one. So even though we won state titles, placed in the top ten each year nationally, and had a personal trainer, we weren't officially a sport. We even had to practice at 6:00 a.m. because that was the only time we could get the gym; all of the "real" sports teams got the gym after school.

I turned thirty-two this spring, and I'm still mad about something that happened half a lifetime ago . . . Oh, wait, did I already say that?

Yup. Sore subject then, sore subject now. I used to defend it all the time.

Everyone knew this, of course. And, being the diplomatic and empathetic high school girls they were, my friends would use it just to get a rise out of me whenever they could. Like that day in English class. And as we sat there, one of the soccer chicks went there. *Again*.

And I took the bait. *Again*.

I tried to explain the training and stamina that go into dance and how I didn't have time to do both dance and soccer.

My argument wasn't working, which shouldn't have surprised me because it never worked. Looking back, it was kind of like trying to rationalize with one of my toddlers, honestly. A toddler in a Catholic school uniform at an all-girls school who's hormonal and needs to vent her frustrations somewhere.

"Yeah," Soccer Chick continued. "You probably don't want to [try out]. You're not really an athlete anyway."

Are. You. Frikkin'. Kidding me right now?

I'm not sure how we made it out of class that day without a brawl, but we did. Also? I was trying out for soccer. That whole dance-soccer-time excuse had just been chucked out the window.

What gets you fired up like that? What does someone need to say or do that will make you drop all excuses and go for it?

That's all it took for me that day, and it's the same today.

The fastest way to get me to do something is to tell me I can't.

The whole thing about not having enough time for soccer? It was an excuse. I could find the time between morning and afternoon practices, but really, I was scared. I knew my skills were rusty and that I wouldn't be nearly as good as I was three years ago. I knew there was a chance I wouldn't make the team.

For some reason, I let myself get away with saying I couldn't do it because there wasn't enough time. I let myself make excuses. But the minute someone else said it? Boom. The excuses were gone.

I tried out—and made the team. Sure, it was only JV while the rest of my friends were on varsity, but I made it. I even took one of the English-class girl's spots on the team.

I did get to play that season, and I did okay. And confession: I never even told my parents, because I would have been so embarrassed if I had not made the team, and then I was afraid of screwing up out on the field.

So this story doesn't end with me scoring a game-winning goal or clawing my way to varsity and a state championship.

Instead, it ends with me making the team *and* continuing with dance. As it turns out, I was laying the foundation for the core principles of the Free Mama Movement.

The Either/Or Mentality

As far back as I can remember, I've known that we humans don't have to limit ourselves to being just one thing. I refuse to accept an either/or mentality.

Dance can be an art AND a sport. And being one in no way makes it any less of the other. Girl, let me tell you how graceful we were *and* how athletic!

I can be a mom AND a business owner—and many other things, for that matter. I can do both: raise my children AND work from home.

You can too, Mama.

You are *meant* for more.

You can hold a video conference in your living room and then walk six feet away to make grilled-cheese sandwiches for your kids for lunch. Or head to an office if you want. Or drop them off at preschool. Or some combination.

It's your choice. Just don't let anyone tell you that you have to pick one or the other.

That either/or mentality is called a false dilemma. It's when we mistakenly believe there are only two options. And it's garbage.

You're in shape or you're not. Democrat or Republican. You can "lean in" or stay home. You agree or disagree.

Where did the gray area go?

Moms are so guilty of doing this to ourselves and being really, really harsh about it. We label ourselves good moms or bad moms, and some of us do it to others, too.

We mom-shame each other about breastfeeding, cloth diapers, food choices, potty training, and discipline.

Let's cut it out, okay?

It's time to ditch the false dilemma. It's also time to drop the compromising, or feeling like we can't do two things well—like be a good mom and make money. You're not doing it right if you feel like you're constantly failing, if you feel like you should be spending time with family while you're at work, and feeling like you should be at work while you're with your family.

You can have a great family life *and* a successful career.

My father owned a business, but he never missed a dance recital or a soccer game. He worked a lot, but when I needed him, he was always there. He made choices—sometimes difficult ones—about where and how he spent his time.

You too can work really hard and also be in control of your schedule. You can be an involved, supportive parent and also miss the PTA meetings.

You can sell beer and also be eight years old . . . Okay, maybe not that. But you *can* be a little girl who likes to dance and who also starts a business and who wears pink tights and runs down the soccer field.

I still get pretty fired up about that dance-or-soccer story, even years later. If you want to hear a good rant, ask me about it sometime!

That story illustrates so many things I'm passionate about. Soccer Chick attacked the credibility of something I loved and respected. I also knew those girls were wrong and that I couldn't seem to change their minds. It can be really hard to believe in something so fiercely when other people don't seem to get it.

If you choose to become a Free Mama, this may happen to you too. There may be people in your life who resemble the soccer chicks. They don't understand what you're doing. Or they don't believe it's possible.

Are you going to let them prevent you from having it all?

Soon after becoming a mom, I knew I would continue to work. For starters, our bills depended on it. More than that, I enjoyed it. I refused to let that define what kind of mother I would be.

I knew it wasn't an either/or choice. I may not have known the false dilemma by name, but I felt it in my gut. It could be this AND that.

Maybe you're a stay-at-home mom and motherhood has taken over a bit of your identity. Every day I hear from Mamas who are looking for more purpose.

Does it make you a bad mom for wanting more? Heck, no!

It means you know that both are possible and that you shouldn't fall for the false dilemma given to you by society or from your family or even from yourself.

So how in the world do you manage it all?

Glad you asked.

CHAPTER 3

The Secret Is to Not Fall Over

I feel the same way about "work-life balance" as I do about "doing it all."

And it rhymes with schmantasy.

Don't misunderstand me, I think work-life balance is perfectly attainable. It's just that as a society we've been defining it all wrong, which leads to, you guessed it, more unrealistic expectations.

Which leads to more guilt and regret.

And in case you missed it, I'm not a fan of either.

You may have heard I'm a dancer, so I know *all* about balance. And do you want to know what the secret is?

Don't fall over.

That's it.

Okay, so you *might* want to look a little more graceful than that to the outside world. But beneath it all? You're constantly shifting the weight beneath you. Grace is really about how subtle you can be with that shifting, doing it so others don't notice it happening.

The toddler stumbling across the living room floor and ballerina Misty Copeland are doing the same thing, just at different levels of expertise. They're both upright, though—and that's the goal here.

When you balance, something is usually wobbling. Stand on one leg and you're probably teetering back and forth a little, with your arms sticking out to either side.

Don't worry about wobbling, Mama. You can handle it, and you'll get used to it. And you'll figure out the difference between a wobble that's about to lead to a fall and one that's just a little shift.

Later on in this book, when we get into the nitty-gritty of starting a home-based business, I'm going to talk to you about pricing your services. I'm going to tell you why I prefer what's called a retainer over hourly pricing. The reason is because I believe you should be compensated for the *value* of the work you produce and not the time it took you to produce it.

Why am I sharing this with you now?

Because time becomes less and less relevant when you're not using it to the fullest.

You could spend four hours with your kiddos, but if you're on your phone and they're watching a show, the quality of that time spent together is rather low. Wouldn't you agree?

On the flip side, you could go for a ten-minute walk with your child and be so engaged in conversation that you create memories and inside jokes for a lifetime.

Balance is about the bigger picture, not about striving for fifty-fifty every day. Your time will never be spent in perfect yin-yang harmony.

You're gonna wobble.

Maybe you planned to work but your child comes down with a fever. So you shift your (mental) weight and adjust. But then the work stacks up a bit, so when your child feels better, you need to shift again.

Or you could be planning an easy day but a client has an emergency only you can handle. Later, we'll talk about setting boundaries, but when it's appropriate, you can adjust and handle that emergency.

You may have to or choose to travel for a week, but then you're more present the following week. If you're traveling for pleasure, I can pretty much guarantee you'll be a better Mama when you walk back into your house and get wrapped up in baby snuggles. Maybe you'll even return with a nice tan.

It's about asking yourself whether all your cups are being filled regularly. And when one starts to get low, how are you consciously choosing to fill it *before* the guilt creeps in?

You have nothing to feel bad about when you leave your kids with a sitter so you can date their dad. Not only should you not feel bad, you're actually directly benefiting them by investing in your relationship with your partner.

We say these things, but most of you aren't implementing them. You've probably even given this advice to a friend before.

Why aren't you taking it?

Are you actively making sure none of your cups goes empty? That goes for self-care, too! We have a bad habit of putting ourselves last a lot, don't we? But if you're not taking care of yourself, you're not at your best, and you won't be able to pour into your family if your cup is dry.

Recently a Mama I coach told me she simply couldn't network in person to find clients. There was no way for her to do it because she was already home with her children.

Get creative! Ask for help! Get a freakin' sitter, Mama!

You have nothing to feel bad about when you leave your kids with a sitter so that you can go to that networking event if you make the most of it. Not only should you not feel bad, but the connections you make could lead to the clients you need to go on a vacation that year. Once you've unplugged from work and created lifelong memories with your kids, those two hours with the sitter won't even be a blip on the radar. Your kids won't even remember, but for you it was the catalyst for something much bigger.

I'll repeat: bigger picture, Mama.

That little chunk of time you take for yourself helps complete your bigger picture. When you neglect your own needs, you take the scissors and cut out an entire section of that beautiful family photo.

Ask me how I know this.

In 2016, my family unexpectedly packed up our "forever home" in Kansas City and moved to Texas. My husband had been recruited for a new job, and it was a great opportunity for us.

It also took us away from all of our family and friends. To Houston. In June. It was a million degrees, and I was twelve weeks pregnant.

I remember my conversation with my husband when I looked at him and said I was going to show up as a different person in Texas. He, not surprisingly, had absolutely no idea what I was talking about but likely attributed it to my unpredictable hormones.

Back in Kansas City, I was like the yes girl, the busiest person you know.

You wanna know how busy? I was on the board for Young Variety, a children's charity; on the alumni board of my former high school; on the junior advisory board for the Jewel Ball, a fundraiser for the Kansas City Symphony; president of the local chapter of FemCity, a professional women's business network; doing wedding planning on the side; and had started freelancing in social media management.

Oh, and let's not forget that one time I dabbled in network marketing. More on that later.

There was even more. I sat down with my husband one day and wrote them all down. It was kind of ridiculous! It isn't easy to give up things you care about, but it's also not easy to do everything.

I'll be honest with you. Doing those things, serving in those leadership capacities—it made me feel important when my job made me feel helpless.

The problem was that none of them were getting me closer to my goals, and in some cases they were actually hindering me from achieving some of them—like spending more time with my family.

I willingly said yes to each and every position I mentioned, and yet, if I'm honest, I probably spent most of my time resenting the roles and complaining about how busy I was. I chose it. And it was too much.

When we moved, I knew it was time to prioritize.

If everything's important, then nothing is. Tough love: that includes your family.

In Texas, 100 percent of my focus was put on building my freelancing business and helping my family adjust to our new home.

That was it.

Anything outside those two boxes was a firm, confident no.

I want to be the first to acknowledge that we—as a society—need volunteers. Having spent all of my twenties being that person, I had to become really okay with it not being my turn anymore. Not right now, anyway.

Maybe you're incredibly involved in your church or there is a nonprofit you have given to every single year since college.

I hear you.

Remember, the secret to living a balanced life is to not fall.

What's causing you to wobble a little too much in your life, Mama? What's full-on about to knock you down to the ground?

I'm not telling you to give up the commitments that are serving you. I am asking you to consider if some of the things on your plate are about to knock you off-balance.

If you've picked up a copy of this book, it could be time to focus on yourself right now. To make sure your feet are firmly planted so you can begin to create the life you want for yourself without the extra wobbles. You can always come back to the rest of the list later.

CHAPTER 4

HAVE MORE BY DOING LESS

Up to this point, we've established that having it all is not that same as doing it all, that you were meant to be more than just a mom or just a career girl, and that balance isn't about equality but about teetering between your priorities so that the big picture is complete and that it feels good.

Now, you might be thinking, *This all sounds really great . . . in theory. How the heck am I supposed to accomplish all of this in the real world when I only have twenty-four hours in a day?*

And the answer, Mama, is that sometimes you have to quit.

My twenty-year-old self wants to time travel and choke me right now. *Lauren doesn't quit! Ever. It's a sign of weakness; it means you have no follow through, no commitment, no willpower. You quit something and you fail at life.*

I may have been slightly dramatic in my twenties.

One of the most important things you have in life is focus. When you commit yourself to too much or to the wrong things, you lose focus. Remember the saying "If everything is important, then nothing is important?" It's kind of like that.

It's like watering down a drink—it just doesn't taste as good when it's weak. And that's a bummer. Give me the margarita I ordered already!

You want your life to be a delicious margarita with a kick. No salt.

And that means sometimes you have to quit. It can be forever, or it can be temporary. But I want you to look at the commitments in your life and make some choices, Mama. Figure out your priorities. Remember, don't do all the things. Do only the things that are most important for you and your family.

Let me tell you my *biggest* quitting story.

Senior year of college: I was dating my then boyfriend (now husband) long-distance. We had met in New York City while doing summer internship programs, even though he had gone to school at the University of Oklahoma and I was in school in California.

At the end of spring break in late March, I flew from San Diego to New York to visit him, taking a cross-country red-eye flight. Then, the day after I flew back home, I had a final interview round with Teach for America, the program where participants commit to teach low-income students for two years.

My plan was to do Teach for America in the Bronx after graduation and move in with him. Living in sin, I know, but New York ain't cheap.

However, the return trip did not go so smoothly. The flight home was super delayed, then re-routed to Los Angeles because of fog in San Diego. And *then* I had to take a cab (life before Uber) all the way from LA to San Diego, which meant I got in about an hour before my interview after being up all night.

Awesome.

I rushed home, showered, and hurried to the school. I was prepared (I'm always prepared) but exhausted and distracted, and I was positive I had bombed the interview. The whole thing felt awful. "Okay," I told myself. "Time to start applying for jobs in New York."

I was mentally scrambling for a backup plan because, for some reason, I didn't have one. I just completely believed that Teach for America was something I was supposed to be doing, and even though I knew it was really competitive, I hadn't considered a plan B.

Who knows how or why, but I got accepted. I would spend all summer training in New York, and then, by the end, I'd find out my placement. So there had been a little turbulence during the interview process, but everything was back on track, right?

Not so much.

About two weeks into the training in New York, I realized it wasn't for me. I had this feeling in my gut that told me I really *wasn't* supposed to be doing this after all. It sounded good, my heart was in it, and my head was in it . . . but something in my stomach was saying "This is not right."

I was literally sick over it. I had never quit anything in my life and prided myself on seeing things through to the end. How could I just *quit*? My head was fighting it, but our guts rarely lie.

The training was in Queens, and I remember taking the subway all the way back to our apartment on the upper East Side and bawling my eyes out to my boyfriend. He was a little shell-shocked and a lot freaked out at seeing a side of me he had never seen before. I'm guessing that was around the time he knew he was going to propose to me someday.

He suggested I quit.

"I can't quit," I said through my tears. "You can't just quit something like this."

But then he made a really great point (one of lots of the reasons I decided to marry him).

"You can either walk away now," he said, "or you can wait until August when you get a classroom of twenty kids and you get attached to them, and then you're miserable and coming home crying every day and there's a strain on our relationship. And you potentially want to quit, except then you have these twenty kids who are counting on you, and a school. You can quit now, or you can hang with it for two years and be unhappy for those two years. Those are kind of your choices at this point."

He was so right.

I thought about it. Was I going to let one terrifying conversation stop me from living the next two years of my life the way I wanted to live the next two years of my life? Was I going to derail the next two years (or more) because of my fear? My guilt? My false sense of obligation?

So I wound up quitting. I admit it wasn't my most graceful resignation of all time. I'm pretty sure I cried, which isn't highly recommended in most professional conversations. But in my defense, I was twenty-two years old and convinced this was a matter of life and death.

And while it was one of the hardest things I've ever had to do, I don't regret that decision for one second. Our guts often steer us toward those regret-free decisions. Do you trust yours?

I know I made the right choice with every ounce of my being. Also, we went and got a puppy to cheer me up.

Seriously, though, I was devastated, but even in the moment, as soon as I had the conversation, I felt tremendous relief. I felt a weight being lifted off my shoulders.

That was my introduction to quitting. That was the first time in my life where I'd truly "failed" at something.

It was hard, but I learned an important lesson. Sometimes you have to get over the emotional complex you have about letting go. It's self-induced. And it's not serving you.

Quitting isn't always about giving up, Mama. It's about simplifying and gaining clarity on what really matters to you and what's going to serve you and your family. It's about saying no to the things that don't line up with your have-it-all lifestyle.

Successful people quit all the time.

They quit doing things that don't serve them, like wasting time or saying yes to things that clutter their schedules, or hanging out with people who are negative.

I have a whole list of things I'd like you to let go of. You already know I want you to quit trying to do everything, but here are a bunch of other things I want you to quit as soon as possible:

- Feeling guilty
- Making excuses
- Putting your needs last

- Procrastinating
- Being overwhelmed
- Being distracted
- Letting people break through your boundaries
- Telling yourself you're broke

I want to touch on that last one for a moment because it definitely hits home for me. I spent years making backhanded comments about my bank account, and I usually did it in front of my husband. Let me tell you, it didn't go over well.

Have you ever read *You Are a Badass* by Jen Sincero? Just kidding, who has time to read? I listened to it on Audible. Anyway, a bunch of Free Mamas were listening to it, and so, in an attempt to stay cool and relevant within my own community, I gave it a listen.

It's a fantastic book, and 2012 Lauren could have really used it in her life. One part in particular jumped out at me: Jen makes a point about self-sabotage and how sometimes we tell ourselves defeatist type things—like I'm broke—because then, when we are too afraid to do anything about it, we get to "win" by being right.

Wow. How messed up is that?

I did this to myself—and my husband—for years. Thanks, Jen, for calling me out on my crap.

Speaking of crap, I have another quitting story, though it's not as dramatic as the Teach for America one. This one's about cloth diapers.

I used them for my first two kids and loved them. They saved me a ton of money, and I felt like I was doing my good deed for the environment. But then my third baby came along.

It was chaos, and it was ugly. Like, literally ugly. It took one giant blowout poop at the park, and boom—I was done. Come to Mama, Amazon Prime! Diapers delivered automatically.

I just couldn't do it with three kids. Could I have found a way? Of course. But it wasn't worth it.

Sometimes your decisions are smaller, like that one, but all those little decisions add up. In addition to the stress of it, those cloth diapers added a whole lot of extra laundry to my day. And the time spent there could instead be spent with family or working on my business.

Our decisions about how we spend our time are a lot like our decisions about spending money. Little choices lead to big results because those little blocks of time add up to big chunks.

Maybe it seems like no big deal to take on that volunteer gig, but what are you missing out on by doing it? You don't have to volunteer for *everything*, Mama! (Take it from the person who used to volunteer for everything.)

You can pick and choose, and maybe your children can help you by telling you what's most important to them.

If you need to bring in money, volunteer work isn't getting you there, noble as it may be. Focus on your finances, get the money pressure off, and *then* add things back in. Volunteer opportunities will always be available.

Or maybe you need to outsource a few things in your life. Think beyond business on this one. What can you let go of? You can hire someone to clean your house, do your laundry, or mow your lawn. If you freed that time up, what could you be doing instead? Could you enjoy more family time or have more time to find clients?

And some things you just need to quit. If it doesn't bring you happiness or leaves you feeling overwhelmed or exhausted, think about quitting.

I want you to think differently, Mama. Spend some time examining your priorities and how you spend your time. You can always adjust. Remember balance? You're going to constantly evaluate how things are working and what needs to be added or deleted.

But the days when you thought you had to do more to have more? Those are gone.

Section 2

You Are Your Greatest Asset

CHAPTER 5

Moms Who Work

For as long as I can remember, I wanted to be a mom.

The house I lived in from age five to about fourteen was my parents' dream house. My dad built it with a huge playroom that had these little alcoves. One was our dress-up alcove, another was staged like a little classroom, and there was another where we'd play house.

I always wanted to be the mom when we played house. When I got older, I became a mother's helper and a babysitter, and I always wanted to be around little kids.

I'm sure a big part of that was because I had a great mom growing up (to be fair, she's still pretty awesome). It could also have had something to do with my desire to always be in charge. Who knows?

My mother was a stay-at-home mom and also one of the most engaged people I knew. She volunteered and was out in the community all the time, plus at the school whenever we needed her.

Have you ever heard the saying "If you want something done, ask a busy person to do it"? That was my mother. People loved my mom, who was the busiest stay-at-home mother ever. She was *the* yes girl, and I both thank her and curse her for passing along this trait.

She was a tremendous example of what motherhood could look like, and so, of course, I assumed I'd do things the same way.

But by the time my first child, Daphne, was born in 2012, I knew I wouldn't be a stay-at-home mom. In fact, it wasn't even a part of the conversation—one look at our bank account told us otherwise. My husband and I never even had a discussion about what it might look like if I stayed home.

That didn't alleviate my guilt, though. Somewhere inside, I had all these preconceived notions (no pun intended!) about motherhood. And it all shoved its way to the surface in the weeks leading up to my return to work.

I took eleven or twelve weeks of "maternity leave," using up all my vacation and sick time, then used paid disability to account for about eight weeks of it. The rest was unpaid.

Aside from the lack of a paycheck, those last couple of weeks were torture, especially the final weekend home. I dreaded going back to work and felt awful about leaving my baby, even though I had a wonderful in-home childcare plan set up. But this was NOT what I had grown up with, and I felt sure it was wrong. Those last few days, I cried and cried and just felt crappy.

And then the craziest thing happened.

We had a wonderful in-home childcare plan set up with a friend of a friend, Ashley, who soon became like family. To avoid a face full of mascara, I made my husband drop Daphne off as I returned to work . . . and felt like a human. I was having adult conversations.

After pumping in the bathroom for the second time that day, I remember sitting at my desk eating lunch and thinking I might always have to do this. Not for money but because there was something about working that was important to who I was. And that it was okay. Daphne was fine, and I was fine. There was nothing to feel guilty about. All of a sudden I was at peace.

I realized that moms work for two reasons: because we have to and because we want to. Sometimes both. And each of these are freakin' fantastic reasons.

I felt all the guilt evaporate when I recognized I was doing what was best for my family and what was best for me. In fact, what we don't often accept is that what is best for us *is* what is best for our families.

I need to work, Mama. I sat down at my computer that first day back to check email and get reacquainted with everything and realized I loved it. It was stimulating and challenging, and I was using my brain in a completely different way.

At the same time, the fact that I loved to work didn't make me miss Daphne any less.

We live in a society that has this Lean In movement on one side, where you climb the corporate ladder and become the CEO; at the other end is this very 1960s vibe where you're only viewed as a good mother if you're home ironing your husband's shirts and cooking dinner every night.

There's nothing wrong with either scenario. What's wrong is feeling like it has to be one or the other. That false dilemma again.

I never felt like I fit into either of those pictures. On the one hand, I'm ambitious and have my dad as my entrepreneurial role model. He taught me to be my own boss and to do my own thing. But then I also have my mother, who was this amazing stay-at-home mom.

Maybe you've been feeling pulled in two different directions?

I'm not cut out to be a full-time, stay-at-home mother. I don't want to climb the corporate ladder, either. And that's totally fine. There is a gray area, and this book is all about finding your place in it.

Working Moms Rock

I think we can all agree that being a parent is the hardest job you'll ever have. I love all my Mamas, but I'm gonna shower a little extra love on those Mamas still working the nine-to-five right now.

Give yourself some credit. A career can be exhausting, and motherhood can be exhausting—and you're handling both.

I know you feel pulled in different directions and are trying to provide for your family emotionally and financially. You're trying to rock it in your career *and* at home. That's a lot.

I understand the guilt, or at least the pressure, for moms to *feel* guilty about working. Someone will always have an opinion about how you should and should not parent. But the fact is, things are different now.

Millennial moms earn less money than moms of the same age in the 1980s, and childcare and education costs are higher.

So unlike other generations, most of us—myself included!—need to work to help pay the bills. But then a third of Americans believe children are better off when the mother doesn't work at all.[1] No wonder we feel guilty!

You've been told that if you put your energy into anything other than child rearing it will be detrimental to your family. But there is no data that shows this is true. Quite the opposite, in fact. Studies actually show that daughters of working moms grow up to earn more in their

---

[1] 2015 Pew report.

careers, and sons grow up to contribute more to household chores and caring for their own children.[2]

Who doesn't want their child to become a successful, cooperative adult?

How Motherhood Prepares You Professionally

Now, for my stay-at-home Mamas. It's about time you take more credit for the skills motherhood has taught you. Seriously. You're a master at negotiating (screen time, snacks, trips through Target). Kids are *relentless*. They practically *invented* the concept of hearing a bunch of no's before getting to a yes.

My negotiating skills with adults got a lot better when I became a mother. After I had my daughter, I valued my time a lot more. If I was going to be away from my family for most of the day, I was going to be compensated properly for it.

Time is your most valuable commodity, and there's nothing like watching a little one grow up to demonstrate it.

Moms are also great at delegating. We quickly learn to let the little ones handle some household chores and to not stress about whether it's done perfectly. If you haven't done it yet, you're probably considering it now. That's a great lesson for business!

---

[2] A study published in the journal *Work, Employment and Society.*

You learn to prioritize—although you've probably been calling it picking your battles. Whatever! At home, that may mean you tune out when your kid starts belting Disney songs right before bedtime as long as he's actually heading toward his bedroom. Or the fact that they dressed themselves is more important than whether they match.

And then there's scheduling. Who's better at this than you? Birthday parties. Doctor appointments. No one shuttles kids to where they need to be quite like you.

So pat yourself on the back, Mama! You've got a ton of valuable work skills already. All you really need to do is connect the dots and put them to use for you. And we're going to cover all that and more.

Create Your Own Opportunities

I get really stubborn when I feel like someone or society is pushing me into a certain role. And I have a theme: if the road I want to take doesn't exist, I'm gonna get a bulldozer and create the dang road.

After I became a mom and returned to the workforce, I was thrilled to be able to continue to grow professionally while learning the ropes as a new parent. But the older Daphne got, the more I began to resent working for someone else who was telling me where to be and at what time and what my goals should be.

Each day, I felt more and more guilty about being a grumpy parent by the time I got home from work and guilty about my husband, who felt nearly invisible as he slipped to the bottom of my priorities list.

Then I got pregnant again.

After Henry was born, I realized I needed to head down a new road. I saw a stressed-out Mama with a mediocre marriage and two beautiful babies being raised by someone else.

This wasn't what I wanted my life to look like. I wanted the freedom to go to the zoo on a Wednesday morning, to prep dinner and fold laundry before my kids and I hit meltdown mode, and to occasionally surprise my husband with a lunch date.

I wanted the freedom to determine my own goals, to set working hours that worked for me and my family, and to work from wherever I wanted. Around the time my son turned one, I had this light-bulb moment while driving home from work one day.

I decided I was going to prove people wrong and show them that you can have a career and a family at the same time. That you can have it all.

And while I hadn't done it yet, I knew exactly how I was going to do it. And this book is going to show you how to do it too.

CHAPTER 6

WHY SELF-EMPLOYMENT WORKS

Now that we've established why working moms rock, I'm going to tell you why self-employment is the best choice for you and the best way to have it all.

But first I want to take a moment to address all those fears creeping into your head, because I've heard every single one of them—both in my own mind and in my conversations with literally thousands of women.

Most of those fears can be boiled down to one thing: security.

Owning a business is not as scary as you may think—I promise.

It's surprising to me that so many people still think of a job as a secure way to make money, while self-employment is viewed as a risk.

You know what's risky? Taking a toddler to Target during nap time or walking barefoot through the living room when the kids have been playing Legos. Checking Facebook during election season.

Self-employment, when done right, is not risky.

Did you hear that? *When done right*. We'll talk a lot more about proven ways to create stability as a business owner.

Self-employment has the potential to provide you with more security than a job ever could. You're in control, and when you spread out the risk—taking on a variety of clients, for example, and booking your work in advance—you set yourself up for a really great career.

That safe job? It's not so safe. It's all your eggs in one basket and handing over control of your salary and your schedule to someone else. And you know I *hate* handing over that kind of control.

If you work because you love what you do, then by all means, please keep doing it! It's good for your family when you are fulfilled and doing something you find meaningful because you bring your best self back home at the end of the workday. And I'm not here to say jobs are evil. They're just misunderstood.

But if your biggest reason to work a job is because you feel like it gives you security, I'd like you to reconsider that assumption . . . and keep reading.

I totally get it: when you're self-employed, nothing's guaranteed. If you're used to getting a paycheck every two weeks without fail, it can be scary to give that up. It seems like you're letting go and just watching that check fly out the window, and you may wonder when you'll ever see another dollar again. Suddenly you picture your family out on the street, begging for food. Or living in a van down by the river.

Settle down, Mama. That's not at all what this is about, and if you follow my system, you'll be relieved to find out it's filled with preparation and planning.

And think about this: nothing's guaranteed in a job either. How many people do you know who have been laid off or through furloughs (which is really an involuntary cut in pay)? I know my family has been affected by this several times, and it totally sucked.

That job can be gone with the snap of your fingers. It happens every day. And then what?

Rewiring Your Mind

Self-employment requires a huge shift in mindset for a lot of people. We're wired to have someone tell us what to do, and this shift takes a lot of rewiring for some—especially if you actually like someone else telling you what to do. After all, that means they ultimately take responsibility, right?

Ouch. Sorry, Mama. I'm gonna tell it like it is.

Of course, I'm not saying everyone who has a job is doing it just so they can have people tell them what to do or that they all surrender control. Let's get that straight.

Again, if you love what you do, you feel fulfilled, and it's good for your family, that's awesome! You do you, Mama.

But if you're doing it just because you're too afraid to try something new and different, it's time to get honest with yourself about that. It's time to stop letting fear get in your way.

That was one of my biggest fears when I quit my job, and it's one Mamas share with me every single day in the Free Mama Movement community: fear of failure. We'll go into way more detail on this topic later on, but fear of failure is one of the biggest obstacles for so many of you.

What if you go for it and fall on your face? Or worse, you fall on your face in front of your friends and family? It's terrifying and potentially humiliating. It could cost you money. Time. Energy. It's the reason why I didn't tell my parents I made the soccer team in high school—I didn't want them showing up to my games and seeing how awful I was.

That's fear taking taking control.

I have a different question for you: What if you DON'T go for it? What if you have all these hopes and dreams and you don't do anything about them? Think about the message you're sending your children, especially your daughters.

Fear shows up in the way we talk, too. Pay attention to your language because your words will tell you a lot about what you're really thinking and feeling.

I see people in my Facebook group who talk about joining my program and say they're going to take a leap of faith. And then there are people who go "I guess I'm gonna take the plunge."

It may not sound like a big difference at first, but those are two very different things, and I've used them both myself.

When I quit my job, I was a take-the-plunge kind of girl. It was like, "Oh crap, I've got nothing left." There's a desperation in that phrase, and it's coming from a place of lack. There's a whole negative connotation there. You're taking the plunge, diving into something with no idea how it's going to turn out and not knowing whether you're gonna succeed or just hit your head on a rock and drown.

But a leap of faith? There's hope in that, and there's belief, and there's forward movement. A leap takes you *toward* something. Faith is the belief that things will turn out well. Doesn't it all sound a whole lot brighter than a plunge? Plunging takes you to the depths, while leaping heads upward.

And yes, there's still uncertainty, even with faith. There's the unknown. Entrepreneurship has a lot of that, and you learn to get comfortable with it and to trust in your preparation. All you really need is a willingness to learn and the belief that you can figure it out.

You don't know how it's going to pan out when you start, whereas you know when you take a job that you'll get your first pay stub in two weeks.

But here's the flip side: Sure, you know you'll get that pay stub—but only that pay stub. There's a limit. One of the really cool things about owning your own business is that you get to be in control of everything.

You can charge ten dollars an hour or a hundred dollars an hour, you can work when you want, and you take on the jobs or clients you want. There's so much freedom and flexibility—but that's also what scares so many people. You make the decisions around here, but maybe you're afraid to have that control without permission from someone.

I think as a society we're conditioned to believe we need permission to do almost anything, especially when it comes to a job: you need to ask for your pay, your vacation time, your personal days—even for your lunch breaks a lot of the time.

It can be scary to break away from that role. You get comfortable as an adult, and suddenly new things look like threats.

But you've done this before, Mama.

I'm gonna take a wild guess here, but I imagine you didn't ask permission to become a mother or check around to make sure the timing was okay with everyone. And you had no idea how this whole motherhood thing was going to turn out, either. But you did it. Is there a bigger leap of faith than that?

You had no idea what your child would be like, how you would be as a mother, how your partner would be as a parent, or how the rest of your family and society would act in their roles. You may have made plans and a few solid ideas, but really? It wasn't all up to you.

I think parenthood is a heck of a lot scarier than self-employment. In business, you get to make decisions and then change direction when needed. There's no off ramp once you become a mom. Full steam ahead.

The MLM Myth

When I talk about self-employment, there's one thing I am *not* talking about: network marketing.

I want to talk about this for a moment because I see so many women—moms in particular—get suckered into a business model that simply doesn't work the way it's advertised. And then when it inevitably fails, these moms are embarrassed, feel like it's all their fault, and that self-employment is a terrible and risky idea.

But network marketing, or multilevel marketing, is not true self-employment. It's hawking product for a company. And while it's true you don't have a boss, you also don't have the control and flexibility these companies promise.

These companies hook you with a story about creating a better life for yourself and for your family, finding personal fulfillment, and having a blast with all of your new, fired-up friends. And then they reel you in with the success stories (that, statistically speaking, are few and far between, by the way).

Who doesn't want that? I got hooked as well and threw myself into one once. I thought it would be my path toward staying home with my kids, and even though it never felt quite right, they caught me at a vulnerable moment—my second maternity leave.

But the truth is, in case you haven't already experienced it yourself, none of the MLM successes made a million bucks selling products for a company. They made it convincing *you* and a bunch of other people to sell them.

Your success in an MLM totally depends on how well you pitch the dream to others, not to mention on the existence—and survival—of the company you represent! That's the whole business model, by design. It's also the reason that 50 percent of people who join one of these companies leave within the first year and 90 percent quit by year five. I fall in the latter. Over 99.7% of these individuals actually lost money.[3]

---

[3] Jon M. Taylor, PhD (PDF) conducted comprehensive research and analysis of the compensation plans of over four hundred various MLM companies and presented his findings in his e-book, *The Case (for and) Against Multi-Level Marketing*, 2001, https://www.ftc.gov/sites/default/files/documents/public_comments/trade-regulation-rule-disclosure-requirements-and-prohibitions-concerning-business-opportunities-ftc.r511993-00017%C2%A0/00017-57317.pdf.

In case I haven't made my point, let's talk cash money. According to an Inc.com article on direct sales, the median income for someone working in direct sales is a pitiful $2,400 a year. Not a typo.

So if you're thinking about becoming a new business owner through an MLM, it's important you understand how it will actually work: you'll be selling the company's product on its behalf, and your recruiter and up-line will earn a commission on your sales.

You *might* profit. But do you understand how small your margins will be?

It's true you'll get a great discount on those rad leggings or that health drink. But you'll also have expenses that may include a website, supplies, investment in the product up front, plus "starter" fees and taxes. And then they'll want you to go to conferences and potentially buy their motivational materials.

So much for that discount.

The other big myth is that you'll work from home. True, you may throw parties at your house sometimes. But as you grow, you're going to drive to a lot of other people's houses to do parties for them and to teach them to do the same.

On nights and weekends.

And the whole time you're doing all this driving to other people's houses, you'll be talking about how great it is to work from home!

Mama, this one makes me sad. And angry. So many women want to start businesses so they can spend more time with their families and instead wind up being pulled away. There's nothing about it that's a work-from-home model, and there's little about it that's profitable.

If you love the product and the idea of growing a team, go for it! But if you're looking to enrich your life and your bank account, I strongly suggest you to consider another option.

You Have Something to Offer

Right now you may be asking yourself, "And exactly what kind of self-employment do you suggest, Lauren?"

In a word: freelancing.

In case that word is new to you, or you're picturing a super nerdy dude wearing glasses hunched over his tech gadgets writing code, let's break it down together.

A freelancer is simply a person who is self-employed and is contracted for service work rather than hired by an employer for a traditional job. Simply put, you solve problems for other people, and they give you money for it.

Ta-da!

I hear from a lot of women who say freelancing sounds great but they have no idea what service to offer. They'd love to be in business for themselves and want the have-it-all lifestyle, but they can't think of a single thing to charge money for. I believe *anyone* has the potential to be a successful business owner.

Need some proof? I've been paid to check emails, send calendar appointments, and make dinner reservations. Now, we've never met, but I'm willing to guess you can do all of these things too.

You don't have to be a graphic designer or marketing expert or web developer to be successful as a freelancer! You've already got skills people will pay for, and if you choose to learn and develop new ones, gravy.

I'll help you break it down later, but you'd be surprised how many things you've picked up during your lifetime that would genuinely help other people and that they'd happily pay you to do!

Think about your past jobs or internships, classes you took, even the kinds of things you've done as a stay-at-home mom. I don't care if you're a high school dropout; you've got something to offer.

People will pay for you to help make their lives easier. Freelancing is all about serving your clients and recognizing the needs out there. It can take some creativity, but coming up with ideas gets easier the more you do it.

You don't need to have an advanced degree or many years of experience in a specialized field. You can even teach yourself all kinds of skills by watching videos on YouTube and then putting them into practice. In fact, later in this book I'm going to recommend it. People have built houses from what they learned online. Surely you can pick up a new skill or two.

You are your greatest asset, so why not be profitable? It all comes down to what you think about it, Mama. Whether you think you can or think you cannot, you're right.

Believe in yourself and your ability to learn and grow, and you're on your way.

CHAPTER 7

It's Not Easy, It's Worth It

Confession: I did not want to spend Mother's Day with my children this year.

Don't get me wrong—I love my three babies! I'm actually pretty obsessed with them. I love being a mom, and I love having a business that allows me to spend all kinds of time with them.

But every once in a while, I want to do something totally wild: not parent.

I want to be responsible for absolutely nothing—and to pee by myself. So this year, a neighbor and I decided we were going to tell our husbands we were leaving them—at home alone with the children.

We planned a day of brunching and pedicures, made sure our husbands knew we were serious, and kept reminding each other how excited we were for our child-free day together. And then we did it!

It was everything I'd hoped it would be. We totally relaxed and recharged.

And we didn't feel an ounce of guilt.

Why am I confessing this to you? Because it totally relates to the reasons why you want to work for yourself—and the reason you decided to open this book.

There has to be something in all of this that's just for you. And this is where I see the biggest disconnect for some moms. They think if they say that why they want to start a business is their children that that's enough. But it usually isn't.

It can be a *big* part of your why, the same way making money can be a big part of it, but neither of these alone is going to carry you through the really difficult times.

Money and children are two powerful motivators, but they usually aren't enough to help you fight through the rejection, the disappointments, and the uncomfortable conversations. And now that you're considering self-employment, it may be a good time to let you know that at some point, all of these things will probably come along with it.

The problem with money being your why is that it's way too easy to find another way to make it. And the problem with children being your why is that it's way too difficult to quantify what that actually means.

If your why is all about money, what happens after you reach your financial goals? Why are you getting out of bed in the morning?

Or what about this: If money is your motivation, what's going to prevent you from getting a job instead of being your own boss? The minute things get difficult, how are you going to push through?

Let me give you an example.

When Things Got Difficult

The summer we moved from Kansas City to a suburb of Houston was possibly the lowest point of my entire life. Besides middle school. And it had nothing to do with the Houston area or even moving. It was all the pressure and circumstances surrounding it.

We thought our home in Kansas City was our forever home. All my family is from Kansas City, and all our friends were there. We had a ridiculously close relationship with our neighbors. Like, TV-sitcom close. Even the ones who were twice our age. So there I was in my forever house and never leaving it or my free babysitters, the grandparents.

Having quit my job there, I was working for myself as a freelancer, and I had clients, all of them local small businesses. At the same time, my husband owned three car-detailing businesses and was physically gone a lot between the locations.

Like many businesses with employees, my husband's seemed to include a bunch of adult babysitting. A lot of employees had a lot of personal problems, and my husband had to handle the fallout. It wore him out.

And did I mention the six-figure small business loan? Yeah, throw a bunch of debt onto the pile of pressure.

Then, one day in April, a recruiter called. He had found my husband on LinkedIn and wanted to talk to him about an automotive job in Texas. Justin flew down for the interview, and when he came back home, we talked.

My husband was thirty-four years old at the time and so, so tired. I think he was exhausted and had lost his passion. And then this phone call came out of nowhere. It seemed like a sign or maybe a free pass.

The idea of moving didn't scare us. We were used to moving, and each of us had lived in various parts of the country. And the idea of trying something new wasn't scary either. We were always doing that and had basically taken turns in our marriage with who was going to be the "risky" one.

Still, this time we had our family and friends and this amazing neighborhood. We had a wonderful support system. We had two kids and, as we would soon find out, one more on the way.

The job offered him about $10,000 less than what we had told ourselves it would take for us to make the move. Justin looked at me.

"But . . ."

And I knew we were moving.

We took off for Houston in June, leaving our forever home, our family and friends, and the best neighbors ever.

It took two credit cards to cover the cost of moving expenses—I love my husband dearly, but he's not the greatest negotiator!—which meant we had maxed them out for the move. My pregnancy hormones were out of control, which brought morning sickness that was actually all-day sickness. Oh, and I had freaky dreams where I'd wake up sweating in the middle of the night, having just dreamed that a tire blew out on my car and we got in a crash that killed the whole family.

Whoa.

Our first weekend in Texas, the twenty-something-year-old son of our new neighbors threw a party until four in the morning. Awesome.

Also, I had only one client left.

My client base had been local, and the services I provided required me to be physically accessible from time to time. When we moved to Houston, I was starting over.

The pressure was on. Though my husband's new job was a good one, we still had our car-detailing business to deal with back in Kansas City and mounds of business and personal debt. I needed new clients, but I didn't know anyone and was puking my brains out the way I always do when I'm twelve weeks pregnant.

And that's when my husband asked the question.

"Do you think maybe you should just get a job?"

Your Why

You probably already know my answer since the Free Mama Movement exists and you're a quarter of the way through this book.

No. As in, H-E-double-hockey-sticks NO!

I mean, I didn't say it that way. At least I don't think I did. I told him that a job wasn't my plan A, and I wasn't finished working my plan A just yet. I had had a taste of flexibility and freedom, and I wasn't about to give that up. Though I don't really like the word *hustle*, I knew I could hustle for a while and make some things happen.

Now I refer to this intense, get-after-it phase of building your business as short-term sacrifice for long-term gain. As in it's temporary.

We had bought our home in Texas for its location. Not just the town or school district but the actual physical location of the house itself. I could walk Daphne to school when she started kindergarten in a year. If I was going to work a job, we might as well have lived anywhere if I was going to have to put her on a bus.

That's not happening, I had thought when he asked. *I'm going to do what I need to do to walk my daughter to school.*

I wanted freedom, flexibility, choices, and control. Those were my reasons, and they were strong enough to fuel me during this stressful time.

Even in Kansas City, I hadn't had my kids home with me 100 percent of the time. It wasn't about that. They'd go to preschool for a few hours a day so they could socialize and I could work. But I also had a lot of annual passes, and we'd go somewhere fun several times a week—the zoo, the library, a children's museum. I felt like I could both really focus on them and have a business.

I intended to do the same thing in Texas.

This was one of the make-it-or-break-it, big-kid-decision-time moments in my business. You're probably going to face a few of those too. What would you have done?

It was also a moment where I had to trust that I could use the pain and the struggles to my benefit. It was almost like I was trusting the universe or trusting the process . . . I'm still not sure which, and it's still playing out.

But if we're not learning from our experiences and mistakes, we're not growing. Honestly, I'm not sure I felt like a business owner before then. I worked for myself, sure, but I didn't have a system in place for a freelancing business like I do now. While the system I teach in the Free Mama Movement pulls from my entire experience as a freelancer and business coach, the meat of it came primarily from the lessons I learned during the months following our move.

I had to start everything over and *pay attention this time* so I could figure out how to set things up so I'd never have to experience that again. For starters, I needed location freedom.

If money was my whole reason, I would have given up and sent out my résumé. Money is money, and I could make it anywhere.

And then I would have been miserable.

Instead, I did a couple of one-off jobs over the summer. I also had a big retainer from my client in Kansas City. And finally, at the beginning of October, I signed three big clients in one week.

It had taken me about three months. It feels like forever when you're going through it, but that's not very long.

Could you focus and work your butt off for three months, even if every day was filled with pressure?

You're going to have doubts, and you'll experience pain and maybe even some failure. You may feel tempted to quit at some point.

What will you do when you feel like quitting? How will you keep going?

I want my control and flexibility, my choices, my freedom. Those are strong motivators, and the thought of losing all of that is what pushes me when I feel pressure. Those things are stronger than any of my fears or doubts.

What is it for you? What is your why for wanting to work from home and be your own boss in the first place? Spend some time on this one until you are clear. This is vital—the rest of this book won't mean much if you don't have the right fuel.

Self-employment is not easy, Mama. But it's worth it.

CHAPTER 8

The Lies Holding You Back

Before we dive into the practical portion of this book, one thing you should know about me is that I'm known for my brutal honesty. I'm a wear-my-opinion-on-my-face kinda gal. Now, we just met, so I'm going to give you a heads-up: I am going to lay some more tough love on you. Better that it comes from me here, in this book, before you get hit with it out in the real world, right? You're welcome!

At the beginning of this section, I told you about the rewiring that needs to take place to go from employee to self-employed boss babe—the shift that occurs when you take control of your circumstances and quit waiting for someone to tell you what to do.

Want to know what else is in your control? Whether you make excuses or not.

Yup. I'm about to call you out on your excuses. Because I've seen them and I've made them, and I know they're what gets in the way of you executing your plan. You can identify your challenge, figure out exactly what to do about it, and then boom—the excuses start and jack it all up.

Let's name some of them and call BS on them together, okay?

But first, one disclaimer: I understand seasons of life. There's a difference between making excuses and going through something big where you may need to take a break or you legitimately can't focus. So it's important to recognize which this is. If it's a season, give yourself some grace and come back to it when you are able.

But if it's an excuse? Time to call it out. Here are the five biggies I hear all the time:

1. Not Enough Time / Bad Timing / Conditions Aren't Right

Let's be real. Was the timing *really* right when you started your family? Every mom knows there's no such thing as the perfect time to have a baby. Even if you went into it thinking you had planned everything out, at some point you probably had a total freak-out. You know you did.

But you somehow figured things out, right? No matter what. It didn't matter how sick you got or whether you had lost your job or just moved, were about to move, or were thinking about moving, or whether you were super busy, tired, or grumpy. You just did it.

I want you to do the same with your freelancing business.

The timing will never be perfect, and you will always feel busy. There are always ways you can fill a day and other things you can do.

Here's the good news: You create time. You are in control of it.

So many people act like they have no control over time, don't they? In reality, they haven't figured out their priorities or haven't stuck to them. That's all time is.

Isn't that cool? Seriously, isn't it great to realize this is totally within your control? Time is all about priorities, so the real question is, what are you doing that's more important?

If you say you don't have time, what is it you're doing *instead of* building your business?

Maybe you can set a few things aside for a while. I stopped volunteering at school and being on all kinds of boards so I could grow my business. I also stopped cleaning my kitchen more than once a day and watching Netflix every day. And you know what? It's okay. Right now my business is my priority.

You don't have to give things up forever. So what can you adjust for a while to create time for your business?

2. I've Never Done This Before

This is kind of silly, isn't it? At what age do we start saying this? When we were young and something new came up, we'd go "Oh, okay, cool. How do I do it?" And we'd ask for help if we couldn't figure it out.

You do realize that *everything* you ever do is something you've never done before, right? Walking, getting dressed, driving, buying a house, making dinner—at some point you did it for the first time.

I understand that things seem more complicated and a little scarier as we get older. But we also have so many resources and so much more experience. Have you heard of Google? And YouTube? And practicing, and good-old figuring it out?

Lack of knowledge should never be a holdup, especially when there's so much information available for free. I get it: we can get overwhelmed. But don't just freeze. Take a few steps and keep moving. You need perseverance to be successful! And if you need a roadmap, I've got your back.

3. I'm Not Good Enough / There's Too Much Competition

I'm talking to you, Millennial Mama. I know you were raised to think of yourself as a unique snowflake. And you are! I'm not here to take that away from you, you snowflake/unicorn/one-in-a-billion you.

It's just, how about you set that aside when you look at your business? And you know something? This is totally okay and actually even a *good* thing.

You want to identify a need and fill that need. If you have an idea that's never been done before, there's a better chance nobody wants it than that you were the first to think of it. So learn to accept the fact that other people are probably doing the exact same thing you're about to start doing.

Instead, figure out how to be the best version of yourself and offer something of value. This is called personal branding. Do your thing as *only* you can do it. That's where the snowflake enters the picture.

4. I Don't Have the Money to Get Started

Don't play the money card with me, Mama. Because I promise you there are people who have been in worse situations and figured a way out.

I've put coaching courses and more on a credit card. I'm not condoning this or even hinting that you do the same. I'm just telling you how far I was willing to go to invest in myself. And it lit a fire for me to get started and earn my money back every single time.

But if the thought of going into debt for your business freaks you out, I'm going to tell you a secret.

All you need is a computer and Wi-Fi. And honestly, you could get yourself to a library for the computer and internet if needed. There's enough information available online to figure out anything you want to learn, and you can run a successful freelancing business with just these two things.

That may sound funny coming from someone who sells courses. But understand what a course is: It's a fast-track plan. It's a method to move more quickly through information because it's all in one place and comes from someone who's been there and done that.

Would you invest $1,000 to launch your business and find clients in a few months rather than a couple of years? That's the idea behind courses. But if you sincerely don't have money to invest in your greatest asset, you can do it anyway. It'll probably just take you longer and you'll make more mistakes. But you can still get there.

The real difference between those who are successful versus those who aren't is their mindset (that word again!). They believe they can and keep going even when things are tough. I can assure you, it is not that they had more money than everyone else.

5: I Don't Know Where to Start

I said it before: Google is your friend. Start Googling anything you want to know; it isn't hard to search. Just type in your question and start reading.

You can go to YouTube and watch tons of free training videos, too. Even better, join the Free Mama Movement

Facebook group and start by watching a few dozen of mine. I even have a live video called *I Don't Know Where to Start*.

And take advantage of other free Facebook groups, too. You can ask any question, and there are people who have answers. Just search the topics you're interested in and see what results show up, then join—and again, start participating.

The best thing to remember is that we all learn best by doing. Not watching. Not reading. At the end of the day, you will actually have to *do* something. You'll have to tell people you're freelancing, and you may need to network and put yourself out there in ways that terrify you. The last section of this book will help you navigate your fears about announcing your business.

The Social Media Trap

This one deserves its own separate section. Raise your hand if you've ever had an experience where you felt worse about yourself because of something or someone you saw online.

Here's my sad social media story and how I used an old friend to fuel my lack of success:

Call it arrogance. Call it luck. Whatever it was, it got me my first "big kid" job after moving back to Kansas City about a month before my husband and I got married.

I scoured the internet for employment opportunities and hated all of them. It was 2009, the job market was garbage, and I was determined not to do something boring.

I decided the whole job-getting process wasn't for me, and I flipped it on its head. Instead of waiting for a company to tell me they were hiring and then applying for a job, I was going to contact *them* and tell them why they should hire me instead.

Having enjoyed planning my own upcoming nuptials and thinking I'd done a pretty good job so far, I emailed KC Weddings. I knew they had big bridal shows every year, plus a magazine to sell. That didn't sound boring to me at all.

As luck (or arrogance) would have it, Gwen Hefner was about to have her first baby any day, and my email landed in her inbox.

Having possibly found her own replacement, Gwen forwarded my email to the publisher. I got the job.

I mention Gwen by name because there's a good chance if you love Instagram and home design you've heard of her, and because while I don't even know her well, she was a big part of that phase of my life. I stepped into a huge role in the magazine division of the *Kansas City Star*, which had five magazines in total. I organized all the events and promotions, same as Gwen had done.

And that was the "problem." Gwen had been amazing. A-ma-zing. And no matter how well I did, I kept being introduced to people as "the new Gwen." For two years, I was the new Gwen.

I also followed Gwen on social media as she'd gone from working girl to stay-at-home mom to internet stardom as *The Makerista*. Her blog, her Instagram, her *everything* was so creative and visually stunning, and she had about a gazillion followers. She appeared to be everything I wanted to be.

I am *not* creative. At least I don't think of myself that way. I have innovative ideas, but I do not—cannot—make pretty things. I'm lousy with crafts, have horrible handwriting, and can't even arrange a store-bought bouquet in a vase without stressing out. I'm a numbers girl. I'm driven and type A and all about systems and time blocking and a go-getter. And Gwen is gorgeous and artistic. And she was doing what I thought I wanted to do. Or maybe she seemed to be who I hoped I could be.

I left the *Kansas City Star*—and the days of being the new Gwen—before Daphne was even born, before the seeds of self-employment had really even been planted in my mind. And yet, over the years, that little voice of doubt crept in and started asking whether I could really do this, whether I was good enough, every single time I saw Gwen pop up on my news feed.

Her photos constantly reminded me of what I hadn't achieved yet or wasn't good at or wasn't taking action on. They always made me feel less than. This was ridiculous, of course—we were different people doing different things, but I kept seeing her and her version of success and comparing myself to it.

As I followed Gwen on social media, that little voice got a megaphone. And I was feeling worse and worse about myself. I mean, this wasn't some Pinterest fantasy. I knew this gorgeous human!

None of this was Gwen's fault, of course. Until I asked her permission for her to be included in this book, she's been blissfully unaware of my own limiting beliefs, and it wasn't her problem to deal with. It was her job to focus on her business and her family, and my job to focus on mine.

As much as I adore Gwen, I have to admit that for a long time I actually had to stop following her on social media because I was hurting myself with it. In a twisted way, I was using her success as an excuse for why I couldn't be successful myself.

It's a fine line between being inspired and motivated by social media and allowing yourself to become depressed over it. I was too hung up on what Gwen was doing and telling myself I could never do the same thing as well as she did it.

Here is what I want you to know: it's up to you to decide how you use social media.

There is no doubt it can enrich your life! You can share photos with grandparents and cousins in different parts of the country, and the world, even. You can network and grow a business from behind your computer. You can form real friendships with people who maybe you'll be lucky enough to meet in real life. I've seen it in the Free Mama Movement Facebook Group time and time again. If you've never been to a Free Mama meetup, you're missing out!

It *can* enrich your life, or you can let it bring you down.

And frankly, it says a lot more about you than it does the person making you feel a certain way.

I was scared and insecure when I stopped following Gwen.

Facebook, Pinterest, Snapchat, Instagram, Twitter—they're just tools. They're like scrapbooks where we paste in our favorite memories and share them with friends. And what do we do? We keep the good pictures and toss the ugly ones.

People show up on social media and put their best foot forward, not their real foot. It's all filtered, for better or worse. And it's up to you to control how often you go there, the people you interact with, and how you allow it to make you feel about yourself.

Being inspired is one thing, but the minute you start to cast the negative on yourself, how you parent, or anything else, it becomes unhealthy. You need to impose self-control and boundaries online as much as anywhere else in your life.

It's noise that is preventing you from becoming the best version of yourself in real life, not in a photo you'll post to your news feed.

When you scroll through Pinterest and see those perfect photos of homemade school snacks and teacher gifts, don't beat yourself up for grabbing the Starbucks gift card in the drive-through on the way in that morning. (The teacher will LOVE that, btw. Just sayin'.)

In fact, there's probably another mom looking at *you* with that Starbucks wondering how the heck you made it out the door in *real clothes* early enough to pick up that bad boy.

You just don't know.

We're all wobbling. Hey, I posted an adorable picture of my daughter on Instagram getting her hair shampooed . . . because she had head lice. I want to bring you the real life, Mama. Can we promise each other we won't get caught up in comparisons?

Comparisons are lies we tell ourselves. And I want you to treat yourself better than that.

Section 3

Setting Yourself Up for Success

CHAPTER 9

KNOWING WHERE YOU'RE GOING

If you're still following along, that means something about the Free Mama life is tugging at your heart strings. Which is great news! It also means it's time to get moving. You acknowledged your excuses and told them to kiss off. The time is now.

The really great news? The second half of this book is going to help you with taking action.

The key is to move quickly. You're going to hit obstacles, but what makes the difference is how quickly you can figure out how to move past them. You're going to launch your freelancing business quite imperfectly. Even you perfectionists. Why? Because it will literally never be perfect. Not your website. Not the timing. Not the way you feel about this whole endeavor.

The mission of the Free Mama Movement is motivating, but tools and templates are helpful for execution. It's time to dive into the systems and strategies that will launch you from dreamer to doer.

Where Are You Going?

Maybe you've heard the saying "A goal without a plan is just a wish."

By now you know that I'm a planner and a list maker and an organizer and a control freak. I'll leave the wishes for when I'm outside at night with my kids searching for shooting stars. Or in the bathroom wishing for alone time.

You're ready to move forward—and quickly—but where are you actually headed? It's important for you to lay out what that looks like for you now, and you'll start by defining your goals.

Goals are milestones for you, targets you set up to gauge whether you're making progress. These are going to be things you can easily look at and figure out whether you've hit them or not.

Think of your goals as an endpoint. Of course, they're not the end of the end, but they're something that allows you to work backward to figure out how to get there. You have to know where you're going, Mama. Otherwise you'll wander aimlessly. There's no point in starting a business when you don't know where you're headed with it. Think of it as setting up the target first and then getting out your child's nerf gun.

Call me crazy, but I think this is where things really start to get fun! You are in control of your goals! You get to decide what's important here, and you control the actions you'll take—or not take—in order to get there.

Do you want to replace your nine-to-five income by the end of the year? Great goal!

Do you want to save up $5,000 for a vacation in Fiji? Get your vision board on.

Do you want to launch an agency that grosses a million dollars annually? You go, girl.

Let your imagination run wild for a moment. Turn off those self-limiting beliefs. Whether you think you can or think you cannot, you're right.

Did you notice something? None of these examples were as vague as, well, the title of this book. When it comes to defining where you're going, it's not enough to say you want to work from home, control your schedule, and make more money. I mean, obviously you *want* these things or you wouldn't be reading! But what do these things actually *look* like?

It's not enough to set any old goal; you need criteria. You've likely heard of SMART goals, but if it's a new concept for you, the acronym stands for *specific*, *measurable*, *achievable*, *relevant*, and *timebound*.

Specific

If you haven't gotten really specific about defining your goal, how will you know when you've reached it? You need to be able to recognize the endpoint.

In my program, I use an example of making $60,000 a year. Let's say that's the number you need in order to leave your job or to be able to accomplish some of your other goals, like that trip to Fiji—whatever it is for you.

So you want to make more money? Great! Who doesn't? You'll need a specific number.

Measurable

Yep, that $60k goal is measurable. A specific number is about as measurable as it can get. And it can be further broken down to $5,000 a month, which lets you then decide what actions to take to get there.

What if it's not a number for you? That's fine. Maybe you want to have more control of your schedule. Your goal can be to carve out me-time for at least thirty-minutes a day. Or an hour!

You may want to quit your job by a specific date. Or land two new clients.

Or maybe you want your kids to start helping out with chores. Which chores?

Whatever the goal, make sure you have a way to measure with tangible evidence whether or not it's a success.

Achievable

Before you roll your eyes, I realize I just asked you to let your imagination run wild, and now I'm telling you to reel it in. There is a lot of controversy over being "realistic" versus dreaming big. I don't think it's one or the other, kind of like having it all. I'm all for dreaming big AND for being realistic. You need to know what steps to take on the way to those big dreams.

I'm going to get totally vulnerable with you for a moment. When I was writing this book, I pictured myself talking about it on the *Today Show*. Seriously! That's one big, dreamy-sized goal right there, and I still believe it's achievable. But I also know I had to actually finish writing the darn thing first.

When you set your goal, make sure it's achievable, as in, make sure you're willing to do the work in order to make it happen—step by step. You want to stretch yourself, but don't set yourself up for failure. Don't make it a goal to make a million dollars if you aren't willing to be a million-dollar business owner and all that it entails. What will you *really* do?

In our example, the $60,000 can be broken down into five clients each paying $1,000 a month for projects.

Totally doable! Will it be challenging when you're first starting out? Sure. But you can see how it's achievable, too.

Relevant

The main question I want you to ask yourself is *why* you want to reach this goal. You want to quit your job, but is it because your boss is a jerk or because you truly want to be your own boss and work from home? You need to know the objective behind the goal and make sure your goal is really going to help you achieve it.

Maybe you want to earn $60,000 so you can replace your income and work from home. That figure is relevant to your life's goals. You can attach it to something that's meaningful to you.

Time Bound

Finally, you need to know how to measure your goal against time. You move forward when you have a deadline attached. I call this "lighting a fire."

If you say you want to work from home someday, guess when that'll happen. Probably never. But if you want to quit your job four weeks from today, you have a goal with a deadline, you're beginning with the end in mind, and you can work your plan.

A deadline gives you a sense of urgency and makes it harder to procrastinate. Even though it's scary as heck, I challenge you to add something super uncomfortable to the mix for an extra flame—perhaps a financial investment in a coaching program or going ahead and putting in your notice with your manager now.

As long as you've given yourself a SMART goal and have a willingness to figure it out, I believe you will succeed in these situations because failure is literally not an option.

Set a timeline and watch as things start happening.

Wants, Needs, Haves

The thing about goals is that you need to be able to focus on them, so if you set too many, you're gonna be in trouble. More than one goal is fine. Ten goals? Not so fine. Actually, that's pretty un-fine. That's like spit-up-in-your-hair-that-hasn't-seen-a-shower-in-days un-fine.

Seriously—you don't want to set yourself up for failure because you're trying to do too much at once.

I'm not saying you won't have lots of goals overall. Remember? *Today Show*.

But they're going to have totally different timeframes, and you do need to prioritize. So your long-term goals may be great, but let's start on something closer to today, okay?

One of the first things you need to do is figure out something I call your wants, needs, and haves because this will help you determine your priorities and which goals to move to the front of your list.

I learned about wants, needs, and haves a few years ago when I took a dear friend to lunch. Michael, a forty-something tech guy who had his own successful business and got me hooked on super nerdy things like keywords and coding, had become a mentor to me. He's one of four people in my life, aside from my parents, who truly filled that role for me.

I believe we all need these people in our lives, whether we're paying them as coaches or not. They know what we're capable of even when we start to second-guess ourselves.

Michael handled a lot of off-site tech issues for the school I worked at before I became a freelancer, and I met him when doing professional development. I remember very early on that he said to me, "You're not going to be in this job very long," and he asked me what I was doing working there before I had even asked myself that very question.

He's the guy who gave me my final pep talk before I turned in my notice.

At this particular lunch, we sat across from each other at The Mixx a few months after I had already left my job. I was settling into my new normal working from home, and while things were going well with my first few clients, money was getting tight. I don't know about you, but my husband and I have a harder time being kind to one another when money is tight.

I was talking to Michael about how I was planning to start a blog, write a book, and on and on, to solve our money woes. All of my big, dreamy goals came pouring out.

He stopped me (no small feat!).

"Those are all great," he said, "and I know someday you're going to go on to do these things. But what about what you *need* to do? That's what you need to think about."

He told me that in order to uncover what I was called to do, I had to align what I wanted to do with what I needed to do with what I had to do.

I was speechless (again, no small feat!). I'd been so busy plotting out the rest of my life I had lost sight of the immediate.

And I admit, I was not super thrilled with that conversation. This was the mentor who believed in me, and what I heard in the moment was, "You're not going to be able to do this." I'm sure what he actually said was, "You're not going to be able to do this right now," but in my ticked-off head, I tuned out the "right now."

By the time I drove home, logic kicked in, and I knew he was right. I had to take care of my haves first, or the rest didn't matter. And that's what I want for you too. If you don't get started on your haves, you won't be able to think clearly enough to get into the rest of it.

I *wanted* to make an impact and help people and share the Free Mama message with the world. But I wasn't going to get there if I didn't take care of some have-tos first. And I had to get our finances in check.

I mean, I *want* Starbucks every morning. But do I *have* to have it? (I want to say yes even though store-bought coffee will also deliver caffeine.) Do I *need* it? (No. And my wallet agrees.)

I thought about what he said and about my wants, needs, and haves.

I *had* to work and to make money because my family relied on two incomes. Now that I'd quit my job, I needed to bring in more money, and quickly. That really brought things into focus. Income-producing activities. The blog, the book, the movement would all have to wait.

It was like a Venn diagram, Michael said, where the three circles overlapped. When you found the thing that met all three, the thing that helped you get to the center, that was the jackpot: when you were doing the stuff you had to do that was also the stuff you needed to do and also the things you wanted to do.

The have-it-all lifestyle? It lives in that spot where those three intervene!

Haves

These are the non-negotiables in your life, and the more specific you can be, the better.

If you have to contribute financially to cover your bills, write down the number. This is a have-to. You can't do anything else until you get this taken care of.

Maybe you have to be home with a special-needs child or be available to attend doctors' visits with older parents each week. Maybe your faith is important to you and you feel called to lead your church's youth group.

Like your why and your goals, these are specific to you and your family. It doesn't really matter what mine or anyone else's are. Your haves are unique to you.

Your haves need to be taken care of so you can feel a sense of safety in your life. It's pretty much impossible to think of anything else if you don't have these things taken care of.

Needs

Next comes needs. What does your family need?

Maybe you need more support from a spouse, more professional development, or a childcare situation that allows you to focus on work.

Maybe you're a military family and you need location freedom. This became a big one for me and is now a top priority. When we moved away from Kansas City, I learned that location freedom was huge; I needed a business that could travel with me. Or stay home with me, as the case may be!

Maybe you're an artist and you need to create every day, or a dancer who needs to dance.

Your needs aren't quite as critical as your haves, but they're still pretty important.

Wants

This is where some of the really fun stuff comes in! Like my Starbucks grande iced coffee half sweetened with soy milk. Mmmmm. Want, want, want.

Go for it when thinking about your wants. It can be anything, big or small.

Maybe you want to take a family vacation every year or have more time for fitness. Or you want to hire a housekeeper. Maybe you want the Mercedes and the boat.

Once you get your haves and needs met, these wants become more realistic and easier to reach. It's a progression, and when you understand these categories, you'll understand how to set your goals from short-term to long-term.

The more goals you reach, the more goals you'll set.

Why?

Because you will *finally* start to show yourself what you're really made of.

CHAPTER 10

Hanging Your "Open" Sign

Do you know what a hobby is? Something you do for fun and relaxation, usually when you can find the time for it.

That can be knitting, dancing, writing, or even hanging out on social media.

And you know what a business is? Something you're all in with, that you prioritize, set up systems for, and make an income from.

That can be knitting, dancing, writing, or even hanging out on social media.

The point is, just about anything can be a hobby. And just about anything can be a business. It's all about how you treat it. And whether or not you make money from it.

You *can* make an income from knitting. Plenty of people have done it! They studied the market and the competition, found a need and a niche, and developed a plan. You can bet they're on social media, too, and that they have systems in place.

A lot of people write as a hobby, and that's fine if you want to do it to relax or just because you enjoy it. But thousands of people also write for a living.

The IRS even chimes in on this topic. If you have an accountant—and I suggest you at least consult with one—they'll let you know whether the government considers your efforts a business or a hobby. And you do not want to claim something as a business that the government doesn't think of in the same way.

If you are looking for something to do that will make you happy and fill your cup, maybe a hobby is what you're after.

But if you're ready to work hard while having a ton fun rocking out your new work-from-home business, here's what's next.

Tell People What You're Doing

So far, we've talked about setting SMART goals and getting in touch with your wants, needs, haves as you lay the groundwork for your business and your new life. But there's one important thing we *haven't* done: tell anyone.

It's time to tell people, Mama. Start talkin'.

Now, I know you're probably thinking, *Is she kidding me? We haven't even gotten to the chapter on services yet! I don't know exactly what I'm going to be offering. She hasn't explained pricing. She's nuts!*

I know—this can be scary. We want to build this amazingly successful business and *then* tell everyone about it, right?

But how does that work, exactly?

Oh yeah. It doesn't.

There are some really good reasons to tell people about your plans, and it's not only about drumming up business (although you'd be surprised how many leads you get when people actually know what you're doing).

When you make your plans public, you become accountable. That's a huge part of the reason it's so scary. I get it! We worry about failing and making fools of ourselves. But if no one even notices? Well, that's not so scary.

Maybe you feel like you already "bothered" everyone when you gave that network marketing business a go. But this is different. You're not asking for any favors. You're not schlepping product.

There's a Laurenism out there in the Free Mama community that goes like this: If you don't tell people what you're doing, how can they connect you with the people you're meant to serve?

It's a rhetorical question, of course. They can't!

But this chapter isn't about getting clients, it's about getting comfortable with being a little uncomfortable, and getting accountable so you give your new freelancing business a real shot.

Accountability has a way of making us more creative, too. When you feel the pressure to succeed, to really make things work, you'll find paths you never thought about before. It's so much easier to give up when nobody knows what you're up to. But when you know you're going to run into someone at your son's birthday party who's going to ask how things are going? Yikes! You're gonna want a good answer.

So how do you tell people? That's up to you. You can say something on Facebook if you want to. In the Free Mama Movement, I even offer templates for this sort of thing. The easiest way is to tell friends and family as you see them. Come on—everyone asks, "What's up?" You have an easy opening!

When I first started freelancing, I only told a few people what I was doing. It got the ball rolling, but it wasn't until I introduced myself to people as a social media manager that things took off. Not [job title] at [place of business]. Not "just" a mom.

Tell people what you're doing.

You'll also tell people by updating your LinkedIn profile or by creating one if you don't already have one. Update information across all your social media platforms to include your freelancing information. When potential clients check you out, you want to make sure they see you're serious about your business.

Announcing your intentions is one of the steps that takes you toward making money and out of the hobby zone (which is like the friend zone but for businesses).

Getting the Support You Need

Here's something else that can happen when you tell people what you're doing: you gain support.

I understand that this isn't the case for everyone, and I'll talk about that in a minute. But many of you will find that friends and family will cheer for you, and some will help out if possible. These are the people who love you and want you to succeed. When they see you're passionate about something and they believe it's a good idea, they're going to be totally onboard.

Here's the key: they need to know you're serious.

I've seen a lot of women who do the "behind the scenes" work to set up their businesses, but when it comes to getting clients—and getting paid—they treat them like hobbies. They keep their services a secret or, worse, offer them for free over and over again.

If you want others to take you seriously, you need to take your business seriously.

Are you acting businesslike? Have you set clear goals and outlined the steps you need to take, announced your intentions, set your boundaries, and set up your schedules? I'm going to help you with all that! But you need to show up with one really important component—attitude.

Not the attitude that your three-year-old gives you (we all figured out pretty quickly that three is the *real* terrible twos, amiright?) but a business attitude. You're the boss.

How do you carry yourself, Mama? What language do you use? Are you apologetic about needing time to yourself to build a business, and do you say you're going to "try" it? Watch what you say to yourself and to others. Do you describe it as a "little" business, or this little thing you're working at on the side?

I've heard all of those kinds of descriptions, and the fact is, none of them sounds like a serious business owner. This may be uncomfortable for some of you because it's a role you're going to need to grow into, but you need to start showing up as that person now. You'll grow into it. Physically hold your head higher and lift your chin. Look people in the eye when you talk about your business. Pay attention to your body language as much as your words.

When people know that this isn't a hobby, they'll stop treating it like that cute little thing you do. Or you're trying to do.

Now, some of you may not be lucky enough to have instant cheerleaders when you announce your business. But is your unsupportive husband or mom or sister or fill-in-the-blank *really* unsupportive?

If they are, I'm sorry to hear it and, yes, you will have some extra challenges along the way.

But often, the "unsupportive" person in our lives is mostly scared. Maybe your family really needs your income, and your spouse is worried about paying the bills. Or maybe your mom hates to see you get hurt and wants to protect you. Maybe your sister has seen you try other things that haven't worked out.

It's a little or a lot scary for all of us, Mama. Remember my story about moving from Kansas City to Texas and starting over? My husband was scared, and I was too. Big-time.

But do you want to know the follow-up story? After Justin asked me about looking for a job and I quite passionately told him that wasn't the plan, he never asked again.

I did my part, Mama. I busted my butt and got clients and made money. So he didn't have to stress out for long, and he didn't need to bring the topic up again.

Put your money where your mouth is.

Are you doing your part? Let's be honest—your loved one's role is not only to support you but to protect you. It works both ways; you support and protect them as well. And protection includes emotional protection. We hate seeing anyone we love suffer.

Show them you're serious and that you're not suffering—and that the family's not suffering—and they won't feel the need to question what you're doing.

Put a plan in place and then start working your tail off. Action helps you tackle fear. And as you find success, you'll have some proof—and then that helps you and your family to relax. You can do it.

CHAPTER 11

THE DAILY 5

I know you're anxious to figure out what your freelancing business is going to look like. Services! Clients! Pricing! Oh, my! Don't worry, we'll get there. Remember, this whole thing is a process, and I want to set you up with habits that will make you successful in the long run.

I'm going to ask you a personal question:

What does your to-do list look like?

Does it look like your preschooler grabbed a pen and scribbled all over a piece of paper? Or maybe it's a list organized by topic and subtopic and then subheadings and categories and color-coordinated tasks, all cross-referenced with citations and a bibliography.

Too much.

I totally understand that your calendar may be color-coordinated if you've got a bunch of kids in a bunch of activities. But that's a family activity calendar, not your to-do list. Your own list doesn't need any of that.

I have a rule I swear by: no more than five items on my to-do list. Wouldn't that be a relief? Just five things! You don't even have to finish them all. In fact, this is the framework for my productivity planner. You can snag a copy for free at thefreeMama.com/thedaily5.

I chose the term "productivity planner" carefully. It's not an activity planner. When you prioritize and keep your list short, you actually get things done—the important things. You plan to be productive rather than busy.

Did you hear that, Mama? Productive, not busy. There's a world of difference.

Busy for busy's sake is when you run around doing tasks with no real goal. For some reason, our society thinks this is noble and that the more overwhelmed you are, the more we should admire you. We reinforce this idea through our advertising and the messages we send, not to mention the pharmaceuticals we promote for heartburn, headache, insomnia, and anxiety.

A lot of people have legitimate medical issues they need help with, but a lot of it is self-inflicted. We live in an overwhelmed society, and I'd like to take it back one Mama at a time.

I think *busy* is a dirty word.

I know I said my mother was the busiest person I knew growing up. And it's true. But she also chose it. She was a stay-at-home mom who enjoyed volunteering and serving on boards, and she was lucky enough to be able to do so without sacrificing her sanity—most of the time. That's what she did; it was kind of like her vocation.

I tried to do the same thing because I convinced myself I had to, and I also had a job. In my case, serving on a bunch of boards took away from my productivity and happiness. For my mother, it didn't.

How It Works

Here's what you do: you write down your five tasks the night before, and you rank them. You can make one list for work and one for personal if it helps. You write down your daily goal and then break that up into five action items, starting with the most important.

Then you get to work. You start on task number one, and you aren't allowed to move on to task number two until the first one is done. This forces you to focus and also makes you prioritize. What *really* needs to get done today? Then do it!

That's going to be the hardest thing in the entire world for a lot of you. You're used to bouncing around from idea to idea and task to task. Or you're writing things down purely for the instant gratification of crossing them off moments later. How is this truly serving you in moving closer to your goals?

Instead, you need to focus. Get that first item done and don't do one other thing until it's completed.

I don't care if you get sick of it, or bored, or start to get anxious worrying about everything else. This is your most important task of the day as identified by you, and it needs to get done above all else.

With the Daily 5, you may have days when you cross off only one or two items. That's it. But guess what? If you're like most Mamas I work with, those two items are likely the ones you would have procrastinated for weeks. And they are the ones that matter most when it comes to your overall success.

Here's something else: you'll get used to it really quickly, and you'll actually like this approach if you stick with it. It takes time to build a habit, so don't just try it on for a day. Really commit. You know without a doubt that you're working on the right things, and that keeps your need to do a bunch of meaningless tasks in check. You won't be distracted thinking about a bunch of other things because your mind will be focused on the one thing you absolutely must do at that moment.

You'll be a machine, Mama. More than you already are.

One of the most difficult decisions I made in my business was when I let a really good client go, one I considered a friend. The trouble was, I found myself working ten hours when I wanted to limit it to three or four a day.

Yep—three or four hours a day. Does that make you cringe? Do you feel yourself resisting the idea that any successful, profitable business can actually function on three or four hours a day? Are you flat-out calling me a liar, liar pants on fire?

I'm insanely good at focusing, Mama. Not gonna lie. That's the secret.

You can totally run a successful business in three or four hours a day. Now, disclaimer: you may not *start* that way. You may very well need to put in more time up-front as you build it and learn and put everything in place.

But after that initial hustle? You can get to work for just a few hours a day . . . if you get really, really good at focusing.

Have you ever noticed how much work you get done when your boss moves a deadline up? It's crazy, isn't it? Or how quickly you can straighten up the house when company is coming over?

What if we focused like that all the time? You don't want the stress and the overwhelm, of course. But what about that ability to zero in on the right tasks and get them done?

That's what the Daily 5 helps you do. You'll find you get way more done in less time when you've figured out what your most important jobs are and then focus on them one at a time.

You can't multitask, Mama. I know you can juggle three kids at once, but your brain honestly can't multitask. Even when you change a diaper while brushing your hair and putting on makeup (okay, who are we kidding? You're not putting on makeup), you're not multitasking. You do a lot of things on autopilot and with muscle memory—I've nicknamed this "intentional multi-tasking," and moms are freaking awesome at it.

Intentional multitasking is not multitasking. It's your brain doing something automatically, without you consciously thinking about it. You simply can't go into business-level focus on two things at once.

It also takes time to shift from one train of thought to another and then to get fully engaged in it. Science shows we do best when we focus on one thing and see it to completion, not when we try to do multiple things at once.

As you use the Daily 5, you'll track your progress. How many of the tasks did you complete? Anything you didn't finish gets added to the top of the list for tomorrow. You'll make a note of your distractions and reflect on them so that you continue to improve.

Do you want to know what's a really great byproduct of all this? You totally won't feel any guilt. Can you imagine a world without so much mom guilt? It exists!

Because you've figured out your priorities and ranked your tasks, you'll know at the end of the day that the important stuff got done. Anything that's unfinished was just not that important—and that's totally cool. You can have a four-hour workday because you know the stuff left undone was probably busywork anyway.

Block Your Time

The Daily 5 works well because it forces you to home in on a small number of significant tasks, which keeps you focused and declutters your brain. But there's another component of it, too: time blocking.

Time blocking is one of the greatest inventions ever. Like, even better than Starbucks (though it's close).

Just as you made sure you chose your tasks carefully, you'll also plan your day carefully. You'll know what gets done when. You'll set up blocks of time for finding clients, for office hours, for writing, for bookkeeping, or for whatever it may be.

Stay true to your Daily 5 and set your time blocks to match. Google Calendar is a great place to time block. Plus, it's color coded.

For example, if your top Daily 5 for the day is to reach out to someone about an upcoming event but you put your office-hours time block after your client-prospecting time block, switch that stuff up. You're the boss. You're in control.

And finally, be careful about overbooking yourself. We often overestimate how much we can accomplish in a couple hours or we forget to account for all of the little things that can go wrong or come up unexpectedly and cause delays.

My friend, fellow freelancer, and copywriter extraordinaire Abbi says your calendar should not be an aspirational document. This is real life, Mama. If you have two hours' worth of work, block off MORE than two hours in your calendar. Think about it: you may need to use the bathroom, reheat your coffee for the fifteenth time, stand and stretch, or clean up the hairball your cat puked up. We very rarely get two hours of completely uninterrupted work time. It's just not a thing.

Set up some buffers within those time blocks, and if you finish early, great! Reward yourself with a quick scroll through Instagram. Chances are, though, that you'll use your "extra" time more often than you think, and you'll be glad for those buffers.

Ready for more? In the next chapter, we'll dive even deeper as we talk about setting boundaries. This is what will help you focus even more as you lay the foundation for a successful business.

CHAPTER 12

PROTECT YOURSELF

At some point, you'll need to have "The Talk" with your children. You don't need to get into explicit detail; you should make it age appropriate, and if possible, it would be great for your partner to participate in the discussion. But your kids are definitely going to need to hear this.

I'm talking about Mommy's new business.

(What did you think we were talking about?)

This chapter's going to cover boundaries, and in each related category, communication is crucial. You'll get a lot more cooperation when you're clear in your message and when you're consistent. Your kids will also be much more open to the boundaries you set when they see how it benefits them and when you're fair but firm.

Stand your ground, Mama. As much as anything else, your business depends on this. Your livelihood depends on it. Remember in the last chapter when I asked you whether you were acting apologetic? Boundaries will wipe all that out.

Boundaries are going to help you reduce distraction and get more done, plus they'll raise the level of respect you get. You need to establish yourself as a serious business owner in your own mind and in your own house before you can convey that image to anyone else, like a prospective client. Make sure you nail this one!

So—The Talk.

It doesn't need to be complicated. You can sit your kids down and tell them Mommy has started a new business from home, letting them know there are going to be times you need to stay focused on that. You can tell them that there are other times you'll just be Mommy and that you'll be there for them.

The important thing is to communicate that your focus will be on either but not on both at the same time. This is where it's going to be critical that you follow through!

Your kids will buy into this a LOT more easily when they know they'll have your full attention when it's their turn; if you end up checking email and being on your phone when you should be participating in the seventeenth rendition of Baby Shark, they're not going to respect your work boundaries. You need to show your family you'll give the same respect you're asking them to give your business.

This isn't to say children will fall in line all the time. Please! That's like saying they'll eat their vegetables just because they've been told green stuff is healthy or that they won't leave their underwear on the living-room floor and run around the house pants-less while you're doing a Facebook Live.

But I promise you that you'll have a much better chance at things going smoothly when you lay down some ground rules and then prove to them that it works.

If your kids are a little older, you can even get into the money aspect of things. I talked to my kindergartner about why we need money and what it allows us to do. I think it's important for kids to learn about money and to be comfortable talking about it, so here's a great way for you to start those conversations.

Most importantly, let your kids know they're a part of your team now and that you need their support. Make up some business T-shirts for the whole family if you want and business expense it. Tell them you need their help so you can do your best.

Try Not to Control Everything

Here's the thing, Mama: you may need to let things get a little messy in order to grow your business. I mean, physically, literally, *messy*.

Just like you can't do all things, you can't control all things. Sometimes, to get the best leverage in your business, you'll need to let go of how things look.

This means that if you need to give your kids an activity they can do quietly so you can buy yourself an hour or fifteen minutes—or whatever's realistic—you may need to let go a little and let them make a big mess. That could mean they have Play-Doh time or create some artwork that gets paper and glitter all over the place.

You can't go around cleaning up after them and also work on your freelancing at the same time. I know this is going to be difficult for my clean freak, type-A Mamas out there. Don't worry. You can still scrub the place down—just AFTER you focus on your business.

It's a trade-off. You need to do whatever you need to do to keep them quiet and focused. But if you think your children are going to sit quietly at their own desks while you sit quietly at yours . . . you're either setting yourself up for failure or your kids are aliens. Sorry.

Types of Boundaries

When we set boundaries, we're defining what is and what is not acceptable in our personal and professional lives. And our boundaries help limit distractions; we set ourselves up for success rather than attempting to fend them off as they happen.

I get it. This can be tough. We get pulled in so many different directions, and we sometimes feel guilty when we can't be everything to everyone at every moment. It's time to ditch that guilt, Mama. It's simply not serving you.

Remind yourself that it may be tough in the short-term but that your family is going to adjust and this will be better for everyone in the not-so-long run.

I also think it's especially important if we have daughters that we teach them about boundaries. When they see their mothers standing firm and strong, they will model that behavior. And don't we want to raise girls who grow up to be strong, independent women? Let's think about the messages we send!

In your freelancing business, you'll have several types of boundaries: individual, physical, and time. Let's talk about what that means for you.

Individual boundaries

These are theoretical. This is where we establish the difference between those we live with and those we work with. It's important for us to have these categories because it helps us set up the other boundaries and to plug times and tasks into those "buckets."

For the most part, this one will be really clear. You'll have clients and other business relationships, and then you'll have family and friends. It's true that sometimes family and friends wind up working with you or that business relationships turn into friendships. I know several Free Mamas who launched their freelancing business with a sister or mom. I know another woman who was recently hired by her dad. That's great! But you'll still need to set boundaries—like a rule that there's no business talk at family dinners or no personal chatter during weekly client calls.

One of the more challenging metaphorical "lines in the sand" to navigate may be with soon-to-be clients. Are you communicating your availability and accessibility? Do they expect you to answer immediately every time they text? I've heard that people will treat you how you let them, and in my experience, this happens to be very true. Set up some good boundaries and communicate them clearly while being mindful of your clients' expectations of you.

This next one may seem obvious, but you need to have a plan with your spouse, too. Be transparent about what help you'll need from your partner and whether you'll need additional childcare for your other kiddos to allow more time for you and baby.

When you set boundaries, one of the wonderful results is that you are more present in each, which means you reduce or even eliminate guilt. You are 100 percent there for your kids instead of thinking about work or even trying to do work while with them. And when you're working, you feel good about the fact that you gave your kids your undivided attention, so you can concentrate without distraction on business.

Physical Boundaries

These are literal boundaries, like the way you set up your house in order to get work done.

You need to set up a designated work space and then rules about that space. The best scenario is when you have an enclosed space, like an office with a door that shuts. And locks. Preferably with a dead bolt and a secret password to unlock it. And soundproofing.

Okay, you don't have to go that far. But it's really, really important you have a designated workspace, whatever that means for you. An office is great. If you don't have an extra room, you'll need to find a space you can claim as your work space, even if it's only during designated hours. And then you need to make sure everyone understands the rules about Mom's Work Space.

If you're able to close a door, everyone needs to know they can't enter at certain times. I have an office with two doors—yes, it's a nightmare—but my kids know that when those doors are closed, they can't barge in. Mommy is working, and they can't come in without permission. If the doors are open, they can come and go (within reason).

Do they still sometimes hover? You betcha. I sometimes see little noses pressed up against the glass, fogging it up. But for the most part, they understand the rules and keep out. At least until my one-year-old can reach the doorknob.

Another physical boundary includes my desk. Anything on my desk is off-limits. I don't care if it's a piece of cake from my son's birthday party and it's got his name on it and a candle sticking out of it. NO TOUCHING.

(I wouldn't be that mean. Usually.)

The thing about physical boundaries is that you also have to make sure you don't do work in areas that aren't designated for it. The living room is a family space, and no matter how tempting it is, you don't bring your laptop in and start doing work while sitting on the couch if your kids are around.

Do the lines blur sometimes? Of course. I've brought my phone to the playground and worked while my kids ran around. If I was going to sit and do nothing anyway, I might as well get work done.

Most days, however, I have a physical boundary with my cell phone because, like a lot of us today, I'm addicted to it. If my phone is within reach, I will reach for it. Sad, but true. And, yet, because I'm aware of this horrible habit, I have blocked hours of the day where it goes on the loading dock and I leave the room. It takes self-awareness and self-discipline, but by establishing boundaries and sticking to them, you will become more present in each and every moment.

Physical Boundaries with Kids' Spaces

When you have really young kids or babies, you can work around their sleep times. I know, I know! This sounds like that crappy advice other people give you: "Just sleep when the baby sleeps." But I could never do that anyway.

Seriously—if the kid isn't crawling, you've got some options. It's easy-peasy while they're still in a crib. You can set up a playpen in your work space and give them a variety of toys that will keep them happy. Here's a secret: you don't have to entertain them 24/7! In fact, it's good for kids to learn how to play by themselves; they develop better imaginations and problem-solving skills.

When my youngest became mobile and dropped that beloved second nap, I'd set her up in my office with the doors closed and dump a bucket of toys on the floor next to me. I'd place baskets of my office supplies higher up on the desk. I knew her space was childproofed and safe, and she could play in there while I worked for a period of time.

You can also set them up with an activity you know they'll enjoy. When my oldest was home for the summer, I would schedule all my meetings back-to-back within a two hour period and let her cash in her TV time for the day with a movie.

Find what works for your family. Your business is worth it.

I understand. You just want to get three hours of uninterrupted quiet time, which you're probably not going to get unless you have childcare or your kids take blissfully long naps. It's going to be on you to focus like you may have never focused before, Mama. But if you've got forty-five minutes at a time, what can you do with it?

Personally, I've always used part-time childcare, even after I left my nine-to-five. This was the solution for my family, but it may not be the solution for yours. Between a few hours of pre-school and a good napper, I was able to carve out enough hours each day to build momentum.

The key is productivity and focus, not more and more hours.

A last note on this: if your baby constantly needs to be held, or if a younger child simply can't play on their own for a designated amount of time, you may need to enlist some extra help. Remember, you're running a business that's going to benefit everyone. It's not on you to do everything. Consider a mother's helper, a preschool program, a neighborhood co-op, or a family member. Get creative in finding ways to make this work for you. Create your own opportunities.

Time Boundaries

This can be the hardest one for people because it requires the most self-discipline. Time boundaries means you set up times for work and times for yourself. And you don't blend them.

If you tell your client you will get back to them tomorrow, you don't need to reply to that midnight email. If you've decided that 7:00 a.m. to 10:00 a.m. is work time and you head into your office, you don't also check personal email while there. Or leave the room to do laundry. Or text a friend.

I'll be honest—I never understood the desire to clean the kitchen instead of working on my business. I'm not getting paid to do dishes! I'm going to work on something that gives me cash, y'all.

Try asking yourself that question: Does this activity make me any money? If not, leave it for another time.

The best time to do those household chores is by combining them with family time. Clean the bathroom during bath time. Do the laundry while the kids are doing homework or, better yet, get them to help you out! Even my one-year-old can pick her clothes out of the pile, and it's great for learning about colors and matching.

Take some of the pressure off yourself to get it all done. We involve everyone in chores, so the kids help unload the dishwasher, take the trash out, and do other things around the house. Even really young kids can help by putting their toys away and their dirty clothes in the hamper.

That's another type of boundary: Mom's to-do list! Get the whole family onboard. They all live there too, right?

Don't be a martyr. Start teaching your kids about responsibility and watch your own list of duties shrink. You can thank me later.

If you really feel drawn to some of those tasks, set a time block for them. You want to take short breaks each hour anyway, so tell yourself you can load the washing machine during your work break. Taking that thought out of your mind allows you to focus better.

Of course, doing laundry or dishes or deciding you suddenly need to alphabetize the DVDs is also a form of procrastination. If that's the case, you need to get real with yourself. Are you trying to avoid something unpleasant or difficult? Are you just stuck?

If it's unpleasant or difficult, the best way to handle it . . . is to handle it. Get 'er done. It's a lot harder to postpone the difficult decision and then have it on your mind all day than it is to tackle it as soon as possible and be done with it. Done is better than perfect.

If you're stuck, maybe you can find another business task to work on. Maybe you can ask for help or write down a list of possible solutions. Sometimes you really do need to clear your mind by stepping away from one thing and working on another. You're the only one who really knows whether that's the case.

The Unexpecteds

You're all set. You have a designated work space, a designated work time, and everyone understands the rules. Thing are humming along for a couple of weeks.

And then your youngest starts throwing up. And the oldest is crying about a toy he broke. And your husband is out of town.

It will happen. Well, maybe not this exact scenario, but something unexpected will come up. Breathe.

If you've done well so far at sticking to your schedule, things like this shouldn't throw you into a tailspin. Maybe you stay up late to work on business and you lose out on some sleep, yes, but your whole business isn't going to tank.

This is when you remind yourself why it's great to work from home. You can be there to comfort that sick child. Is the barf in the carpet still gross and the idea of coming down with a twenty-four-hour bug yourself still stressful? Of course. And now that you're self-employed, you have the flexibility to adjust and get your work done at another time.

It's all about how you frame it, Mama! These things are unexpected and inconvenient, but they're also exactly why you're here.

Give yourself some grace. You're doing something special.

CHAPTER 13

SYSTEMS

Some people dream of world peace and of a planet where there is no sickness or strife.

Those are all great. But me? I dream of a world of Free Mamas. And in that world, everyone has systems.

Not only does everyone have systems, they actually work those systems, and the entire globe revolves around order and efficiency. Doesn't that sound amazing?

Okay, you may not be as compulsive as I am—yet—but here's something to consider: systems create more time for you. Yes, Mama—time! Take a nap in it if you want to! Take a shower! Snuggle your baby! Make more money!

I've never met a mother who didn't want more time, and while I'm fully aware that there are only twenty-four hours in a day, I know how to create more of it: systems.

Systems are where you break down and deconstruct your processes, which means they can be replicated, delegated, and automated. It's amazing. When you have systems in place, it means others can step in and do what you do. Imagine that: in a way, you can be cloned!

Systems mean it's not on you to get everything done because you have step-by-step instructions others can follow. You set checkpoints and outcomes and you define the beginning, middle, and end. The result? You save time, energy, and money.

You can do this in your personal life and in your business life. Your morning routine is a great example. So many people say their mornings are chaotic and stressful and that it's the mom who bears the weight.

But it doesn't need to be that way.

You can help yourself out by establishing a morning routine. Even the little ones can get involved. When my son was three, he could get himself dressed, feed the cat, and take out the recycling. There are three fewer jobs for you.

My husband makes breakfast. My school-aged daughter makes her own lunch, with guidelines on what her choices should include. Now there are five fewer jobs for you to do. How much time have you saved already? What else are you able to do because you're not doing those five chores?

Let's be clear about something—this didn't happen organically. I had to ask my husband to be in charge of the food so I could focus on the baby. We worked with our daughter on what a healthy lunch looked like and moved storage containers around so she could reach them on her own. We showed my son how to scoop food into the cat bowl. We took the time to put systems in place, and we worked on them daily until it became a routine habit.

Checkpoints and outcomes? With my son, we'd keep an eye on him to make sure he took the recycling all the way out to the barrel and that he actually dumped the contents into it. And that he didn't dump the recycling basket in as well; then we'd make sure he brought the basket back in and put it away. The chore was finished when it was put away. Beginning, middle, and end.

Does he do it as well or as fast as I would? No. Same thing when my daughter makes her lunch. But that's not the point. The point—in addition to them learning responsibility—is that I'm handing those jobs off to someone else.

Sometimes we don't give our family members enough credit for what they can do. Remember, too, that you're teaching them to feel empowered and self-sufficient when you give them jobs to do and when you set expectations.

And if you don't create processes that allow other people to step in, you'll forever be doing everything for yourself, which is a really stressed-out place to hang out.

Set Up Systems Now

It's important for you to set up systems for your business now, before you have any clients. When you start taking on work, you'll drive yourself crazy if you don't have systems in place.

And if you still have a nine-to-five, you'll drive yourself extra crazy by taking on an additional workload without any systems. You'll soon get overwhelmed and, even worse, will probably fall behind, if not throw in the towel. And that's so not the point of being a Free Mama.

The other thing to remember is that systems are something of value you can offer clients. The key is to review your systems and make sure you have the least number of steps possible to successfully complete a specific task. Reduce those steps while still getting the same result and providing the best quality.

Don't be afraid to ask your client for a training video, which you can then document and write out the steps involved so you know exactly how to do the job. Then voilà! You're on your way to creating a training manual other people can use; you can make a video or a step-by-step guide with bullet points or numbers.

This is also referred to as a standard operating procedure, or an SOP. It's like a list of checkpoints for getting a job done. If you've ever flown, you've seen and heard pilots use SOPs before takeoff. They go through the same steps, in the same order, each time. "Flight attendants, prepare for takeoff." Sound familiar?

You want to be just as meticulous. If you can't do it for yourself, do it for me. It would make me *so* happy. Or do it for your family.

I'm not gonna lie, Mama: systems at home take a little bit longer to set up. It'll take practice to figure out how much time different tasks take and how to handle the unexpected. Plus, when you transition out of your day job and into your work-from-home life, you'll have to reevaluate systems that may have previously worked if they're no longer serving you.

There are some things you can do to make this easier.

First, set office hours. It doesn't matter if you don't have an actual office; this is the first step. Remember the chapter on boundaries? Office hours fits into that.

Set some times when you can concentrate on work—and only work. During office hours, you're not checking personal email, personal Facebook, or paying bills. You're in your designated spot, focused on business.

This is something I'm pretty superhuman at (and modest about). When I'm in my office, my game face is on. Before I sit at my desk, I always make sure I have a water and a coffee. The first few times I may have found myself bouncing back into the kitchen every few moments because I forgot something, but now it's a routine. I'm not tempted to do laundry or empty the dishwasher, and honestly, I don't understand why people are. I'm not being paid for that! Why would I go do something I'm not getting paid for during my office hours? This isn't a hobby.

Batching and Automating

Two of the sexiest words in the English language: batching and automating.

This is my secret sauce, Mama! This is how you get *more* done in *less* time, and when you combine batching and automating with systems, you are well on your way. I want to be super clear that while this section is going to teach you a lot of shortcuts for your business, it should never, ever be at the expense of the quality of your work. This is super important.

First, a couple definitions.

"Batching" is when you block off a chunk of time (time block) to focus on one *type* of task. The idea is that by working on similar items, you'll focus better and get more done. When we jump from topic to topic, it takes our brain some time to adjust; so if you try to do a bunch of unrelated tasks, you'll take longer to get them done. And the quality may suffer too.

You can batch your work by client or by task. For example, you could batch a bunch of Client A's work, which lets you stay focused on that one person's brand, products, and strategy. Or you could group a similar task—deciding you'll do all your copywriting on Tuesdays, for example, even if it's for multiple clients.

"Automating" is a way to get a boatload of work done without having to manually do it all. Hands off? I'm in!

Here's an example: social media scheduling. You should *not* be creating social media posts and posting them in live time, which would be scarily inefficient. Seriously. I just threw up in my mouth a little bit.

Imagine how your day would look if you went in and manually posted items for multiple clients multiple times a day. Let's say they each post to Facebook twice a day, Instagram once a day, Twitter three times a day, and ten daily pins on Pinterest. With just two clients, that's thirty-two items a day, and things will get out of hand in a hurry! You'll never get anything else done and be strapped to your phone or computer all day long.

Instead, you batch the task by blocking off a chunk of time to create a bunch of posts. Then you automate the work by posting times for each of them in a scheduler; the scheduler will post them at the times you pick, and you are on to something else. And if you've written the process down, you can give this job to someone else at some point, if you choose.

Just Tell Me What I Need to Be a Success Right Now

On occasion, a super eager Free Mama will come into our community and firmly say, "Just tell me what systems I need to be successful right now."

Okay, you overachiever, you, I hear you.

Technology changes fast, but I recommend looking into the following software to help you set up systems for your business *before* it's making money. I personally use each of these, and most offer a free version.

- Step 1: Get a domain for your business from GoDaddy. It can be your name. It can be your business name. You may or may not decide to make a website, but you'll need this for step 2.

- Step 2: Set up GSuite. Not only will you look about a billion times more professional using an email address that isn't @aol.com, but you'll also get tons of storage and sharing features with Google Drive, and Google Calendar is the cat's meow for time blocking.

- Step 3: Sign up for free accounts with Calendly and Zoom. Calendly automates the process of booking appointments without having to email back and forth, which you'll need when speaking with current and prospective clients, and Zoom is a virtual video conferencing software. If you're feeling fancy, you can even use GoDaddy to set up subdomains for these accounts.

That's it! Pretty much everything else can wait until you're serving clients and making money.

With these three simple steps, you've created a process that allows prospective clients to engage with you, and it will only take about three seconds of your time once you've set it up. If you can make a first impression that lets people will know you're serious about your new gig and you totally have your stuff together, you'll have clients in no time.

Are you ready to figure out what in the world you'll be doing? Let's go!

Section 4

Becoming a Free Mama

CHAPTER 14

How to Choose Your Services

For a while in my early to midtwenties, I worked a side hustle as a wedding planner. It played to all my strengths as an anal-retentive, obsessive, nearly psychotic planner with a need to be in total control. If I was in charge of your wedding day, that bad boy would go according to schedule.

At the same time, I had no idea what I was doing. This all began back when I was the "new Gwen" working in the magazine division of the *Kansas City Star*. One of my main responsibilities was to coordinate a massive bridal show at the convention center twice a year.

Because of that, I had a lot of contacts within the wedding industry, and when a friend of the family asked my mother whether I could help plan her daughter's wedding, my mom said yes. Thanks, Mom.

The cool thing is, I wound up doing exactly what I now teach women to do in their freelancing businesses: more than simply fake-it-till-you-make-it, I had to rely on skills and past experience to knock down a belief system that was shouting in my ears:

I've never done this before.

It didn't matter that I hadn't done this specific thing. I had all the necessary skills. So I pulled it off and wound up doing a handful of weddings a year.

I was really, really good at it. And honestly, I could have built a business around wedding planning. But it wouldn't have worked for me long-term.

The thing was, I wasn't in love with the wedding industry itself. I was excellent at the organization and the execution around the day of the event, but the rest of it? Meh.

I also hated being pulled away from my family on Saturdays after working all week. It got even harder after my second child, Henry, was born. It was Henry's arrival that really shined a light on the fact that the way I was living my life wasn't doing me any favors and really wasn't working.

That was around the time I sat down with Justin, made a list of everything I was involved in, and started to scale back. Even though it was profitable, the wedding planning was the first to go.

I needed to figure out what I was really good at and how I could make that work on my terms. It also had to be something I actually enjoyed doing, because otherwise, I'd never stick with it.

This is the process you'll go through when you start your business.

Freelancing is all about solving a problem. So we're going to talk about figuring out what you're good at and making it work for you. But just like in my wedding-planner story, we want to find something you also love doing so you're a lot more likely to stick with it.

Start with What You Know

The best thing you can do for yourself is to create a business where you operate in your "Zone of Genius." Sounds a little like a children's board game, doesn't it? Like, after you travel through the gumdrop forest and climb the ladder of life and maybe even pass go, you'll enter the Zone of Genius.

All kidding aside, "Zone of Genius" comes from the book *The Big Leap,* where author Gay Hendricks describes four zones: the Zone of Incompetence; the Zone of Competence; the Zone of Excellence; and the Zone of Genius.

Obviously, we don't want to spend time in the Zone of Incompetence, a place where we don't know what we're doing and are unhappy. The Zone of Competence is where a lot of people feel they are in their nine-to-fives doing something just to make a paycheck but feeling unfulfilled.

And then there's this really tricky area—the Zone of Excellence, where we're really good at something and even happy with it. And yet we still feel like there's more for us but can't quite figure out why. This is where I was struggling as a wedding planner, and even years later as a social media manager.

Enter the Zone of Genius, Mama. This is where your skills meet your passion, where you get paid for your unique abilities and you love what you do!

I'll be totally honest: you may spend time in your Zone of Excellence for a while, and you may even have to start in your Zone of Confidence, because this will undoubtedly be the fastest path to cash in your new freelancing business.

You're going to start with what you *already* know. And that's okay.

Remember our haves, needs, and wants?

Depending on your haves, needs, and wants, you may have to evolve a little like I did. It's important to pay your bills and take care of your essentials, so let's work to get you there first. Then, with the money pressure off, you can get more creative and explore those things that really inspire you until you discover the one thing you can offer that makes work not feel like work.

Five Questions to Ask

I teach seven key categories where you can put your skills to use and where your tasks will likely fall in your freelancing business: administrative, organizational, email marketing, social media management, content writing, design, and websites. The idea is to specialize in one or a few of these to attract clients.

You possibly already know which ones look like possibilities, or you're beginning to panic a little because your brain is asking on repeat what the heck even is content writing.

Don't worry.

You don't have to know everything. *You don't have to know everything.* Remember, I've been paid to reply to emails. You have something to offer, Mama.

We're going to dive into identifying specifics and start creating a niche for you.

It starts with you asking yourself five questions: What day-to-day tasks do I enjoy?; What gives me/gave me the most satisfaction at work?; What tools or software do I know how to use?; What tasks am I able to do quickly?; and What do I do in my free time?

1. What day-to-day tasks do I enjoy?

Some of you will be able to immediately make a list. Some of you won't know the answer off the top of your head.

Get a small notebook you can carry around with you throughout the day and start paying attention. Write down the things you enjoy most, even if you think it's nothing—like cruising the internet.

Those skills can come in handy, Mama! There are lots of clients who need people to do market research for them and who can find information online. So your skill at spying on your old boyfriend's new wife's sister, who you think you saw at the movies the other day . . . use it, girl! Get paid for your creeper skills.

2. What gives/gave me the most satisfaction at work?

If you're still at a job, what do you like most about it? Some of you may have to dig deep. I get it!

Maybe you like working with clients and customers and meeting people. You can turn those people skills into a freelance career in customer service.

Maybe you like technology more than people. Then I *know* a bunch of software programs that would make you geek out so hard, and you probably don't even know they exist! Plus, so many women in business would love to work with a woman who knows her stuff in IT.

3. What tools or software do I know how to use?

In my program, I walk you through the must-have software you'll need in order to wow your clients. Chances are, you have skills you've learned at work.

Think about what you work on each day. If you're in a job, you may use Excel or manage a CRM (customer relationship management) software already. Even you stay-at-home moms probably check your Gmail and keep your family's whereabouts organized with Google

Calendar. These are extremely valuable skills to bring to busy business owners who'd rather work on something else.

And *you* are just the person to help them with that!

4. What tasks am I able to do quickly?

This can be something like typing, which could be a transcription service (there's a lot of need for that). Or that spreadsheet thing again. Maybe you're great at numbers and can balance the books in a few hours instead of the month it would take your client to get it done.

The things you can do quickly will be of high value to you and your freelance business because you want to get in the habit of doing more in less time . . . which means higher pay. I'm going to break down exactly how that works in a later chapter.

That bookkeeping example? Your client is thrilled to be saved a month's worth of torture and is willing to pay for that.

A lot of business owners need content, but they're either not very good at it or, frankly, just don't have the time or desire. They need help with their blog posts, emails, and other writing tasks so they can focus on creating content, developing products, working with customers, or other areas of their business.

5. What do I enjoy doing in my free time?

When you can match the things you enjoy with your business and can play to your strengths, you're going to benefit in the long run. You'll enjoy it a lot more, and you'll wind up earning more because you'll become better at it—and you'll find it a lot easier to spend time in it and keep up on professional development.

So think about what you enjoy doing in your free time. Do you like to dabble in photography and Photoshop? You can use those skills to help clients with their graphics and social media.

There are all kinds of hobbies that, when we really stop to think about it, can be turned into marketable skills.

One last note on this section: you don't have to have it all figured out right now, and you absolutely do not and *should* not try to offer everything! I know that at home you're probably the chief organizer, medic, chef, tech guru, math whiz, psychologist, and plumber.

In your business, you're going to specialize. Maybe not right away, because you're going to want to experience some of these things in your business firsthand. But eventually, you'll pick a skill and get really, really good at it, which will make you super valuable to your clients. Plus, you'll be able to charge more over time.

If You're Feeling Stuck

Every single day I hear from a Mama who feels stuck. I understand. You know what you do now, and you're having a hard time seeing how it could possibly relate to a career as a freelancer.

Maybe you're a nurse and you're not sure how your duties translate into virtual work someone would pay for. Let me tell you—whether you're a nurse, teacher, tractor driver, CPA, attorney, engineer, or stay-at-home mom, you are qualified with skills you already have to at least get started. I say this because I've worked with someone from each of these backgrounds and seen them land that first client.

We're not talking about that $60,000 goal here. We're talking about that first $1,000 client. That's it. The rest will fall into place.

And if you're still not sure what you have to offer, don't panic. It's okay—in fact, it's more than okay. You may not even be aware that the service you want to provide is even *a thing* yet. Some people know it right away; others need to dig into it for a while and be exposed to new things. You don't know what you don't know!

If you decide to begin offering general virtual-assistant tasks, keep in mind that you can totally change it as you go. I started out handling social media management for clients and did well with it before changing my focus to marketing strategy and building funnels, something I enjoyed more, was really good at, and hadn't even heard of until a client paid me to learn how to do it. For real.

I've edited podcasts. Posted stuff to YouTube. Written emails. Approved blog submissions. Built web pages. Managed clients. Booked events. None of these were services I "advertised" or things I was trained to do or studied in school, and yet clients asked me to do them and I figured it out.

The biggest thing is to choose *something* and get moving—and get earning. You don't truly know how to do something until you do it, and you'll start seeing opportunities you didn't know existed.

When I did social media management back in Kansas City, I always felt my clients could replace me pretty easily. Even though I was really good at it, I knew I was disposable. But I also kept seeing other areas where I could help them, so I'd follow up and make suggestions.

In doing this, I became an invaluable team member. Not only did I have more high-value skills, but I became known as a problem solver. Your clients are busy, and it's helpful when someone suggests a quick idea that solves an issue for them. It takes another problem off their plate! It puts more money in your bank account!

If you're having trouble recognizing just how awesome you are, here are a couple things you can do that will point you in a direction (any direction will do, really):

Ask a trusted friend, family member, or colleague what they think you're good at; if you were to teach them something, what would it be? It's amazing how often we can't see our own strengths. You could hear something that surprises you, or you may get confirmation on something you already suspected.

Do a little research. Scroll through your news feed, pay attention to ads that pop up in Facebook, and take a look at your community and group of friends. Who inspires you and makes you feel like "I can do that!" or "I wish that was me!"? If you get the feeling you could do the same thing if you only applied yourself, there's a very good chance this is something you should pursue in your own business.

Find out what services are out there. I'm not a huge fan of sites like UpWork for a lot of reasons, but primarily because of the scammers, competition, and expectation of cheap labor. However, these sites are great for market research. You can literally see what types of work people want freelancers for. Bada-bing, bada-boom. You've already got confirmation there's a need out there for your new freelancing business!

It may not seem like it now, but I had a *lot* of self-doubt when I started too, Mama. I remember being terrified that my clients would know more about social media than I did. I remember thinking, *Who the heck am I to think I could actually help someone?* That's called imposter syndrome, by the way. It still creeps up from time to time.

I think we all live in fear of being found out as a fraud, and we need to remind ourselves that this is just our brain playing tricks on us. You don't need that kind of negative self-talk.

You don't need to be the world's best expert at a dang thing—you just need to stay one step ahead of your clients. Sometimes it's not even about being better than them at all! Sometimes your role is to take a bunch of stuff off their plate and do it well simply because of the time you give back to them so they can focus on growing their business. This is an incredibly valuable service. Don't downplay how absolutely amazing you are at this very moment.

What to Charge

I debated whether or not to even include this section in this book. But because it's a question I get asked quite frequently, I decided to go for it, but I'm going to keep it short and sweet.

Knowing what to charge is a bit of an art. Do you want to know how much something is worth? Whatever someone is willing to pay for it.

You see, it's a little ambiguous. Thousands of you could be reading this, and each of you will offer something slightly different. You'll have different levels of expertise and service different niches.

So here's where you'll start: Do some market research. Figure out what other people are already charging for the exact same service. You may take on your first client for twenty-five dollars an hour and then realize you will never do that same task for less than forty dollars in the future. Good for you! You're learning! You're upleveling! I call this the staircase approach. Sometimes you have to start toward the bottom, but it doesn't mean you can't go flying up those stairs.

You may realize you've got an issue if you keep getting feedback that your rates are too high. This could be because the services you provide simply aren't worth what you're proposing, but it could be because you're not pitching them to the right people. There's a big difference between those two things.

Once you start doing the work, you'll grow into feeling more confident about the value of your work. Which, by the way, is how I suggest being paid. I don't care for an hourly rate, but you may have to start there. The key is to start.

CHAPTER 15

HOW TO MAKE MONEY

Iowa farmer Ray Kinsella was walking through his cornfield all alone when he heard a voice.

"If you build it, he will come," it whispered, and Ray turned around to see where the voice had come from. He had been worried about losing the farm, sure, but hearing voices? What the what?

Whether you've seen the movie *Field of Dreams* or not, you've probably heard that line and know the plot. Ray builds a baseball field on his land—because the voice told him to, of course—and the ghosts of the 1919 Chicago White Sox show up to play.

Later, when Ray's farm is a day away from being foreclosed on, James Earl Jones's character, Terence Mann, tells him that people will drive to the cornfield from all over, and they'll gladly hand over twenty dollars each to look around and watch the players. Ray's farm will be saved because people will suddenly and mysteriously start showing up in droves.

(This is probably why people usually quote the movie line as "If you build it, they will come," even though the word *they* is a misquote. Technicality.)

"They'll pass over the money without even thinking about it: for it is money they have and peace they lack," Terence says to Ray.

And this is *exactly* how your business will go, right? You'll hear a voice very convincingly tell you to start a business. And so you will: you'll build a website and a beautiful LinkedIn profile, and then a flood of super successful clients with fistfuls of cash will start handing you money—because it's money they have and peace they lack.

Wake up, Mama. This ain't Hollywood.

You don't just build something and have people show up and throw money at you. Maybe Ray the farmer didn't have to market himself, but YOU do!

Planting Seeds

You *do* have something in common with Ray the farmer, though: you're going to plant seeds.

In your case, you'll start talking to people and telling them what you're up to. If you've followed my advice from chapter 11, you may be doing this already!

But Lauren, I'm not good at sales. I don't want to have to sell myself.

Don't worry—you'll do it in a nonsleazy, nonsalesy, noncompetitive way. I'm not going to tell you to start schmoozing your husband's boss's wife to sell her a lip gloss.

You're not selling anything or asking friends and family to be your clients. This is more like passing out flyers to your grand-opening event and asking people to bring a friend and check out your shop. This is why you want to make sure your social media accounts are updated and that you've honed your power pitch—but more on that in a minute.

You need to let people know what you're doing. The greatest opportunity could be right in front of you and you don't even know it; people, especially women, like to help each other out and like to connect one another. So when you start putting out the word, people in your network start to think about who else they know who could benefit from what you have to offer. Even better, a business owner may tell someone in your network how stressed out they are, and boom—you've got your first referral! I see this happen all the time in the Free Mama community, and it's happened to me a bunch of times too.

You know who *can't* refer you a client? Anyone who has absolutely no idea you've started a freelancing business. I'll say it again: if no one knows what you're doing, how can they connect you with the people you're meant to serve?

I don't care if you're a homebody who was homeschooled—you know somebody. Probably more than one somebody. Start a spreadsheet in Google Drive where you make a list of people you know—just a list of people you have enough of a rapport with that you could send them an email. This could be friends, family, past colleagues, former bosses. Jot them down, along with their contact info. Facebook messages will do if that's how you communicate with the person. Check your email and phone contacts, too, and see who you can come up with.

The goal is to write down the names of one hundred people, although if that sounds too daunting, go for ten today and get things started.

All you're doing is updating them on what you're doing and asking whether they know anybody you could serve. Customize the email to each person so it's not spammy. Freelancing, like any business, is all about building relationships. So while you're the one reaching out, show the recipient you actually care about what they're up to as well.

Maybe someone will immediately reply with an introduction to an entrepreneur friend. Maybe you'll get crickets. Maybe you'll get an outpouring of support but no leads. Don't let your emotions get the best of you with this one, Mama—you're just planting seeds. You don't know when, and you don't know which seed, but one of those suckers will eventually grow into a client that is going to give you cash money.

Online Dating for the Business Set

When you approach potential clients online, you've got one goal: for them to swipe right and then ask you out.

But just as with dating, this will take a little time. You need to have some back-and-forth, some initial attraction, a little wooing. Yeah, I said wooing.

You also need to be clear about your services—whichever ones you're going to lead with—and know what problem you can solve for the prospective client. And, the same way you may head to a location where your ideal date could be hanging out, you'll start hanging out in places your ideal client would be.

"Ideal client" is fancy talk for the kind of person you want to work with in your freelancing business. It could be people from a particular industry, such as real estate or health and wellness. It could be female business owners, or attorneys, or coaches.

You'll also need a pick-up line.

Now, you've probably heard of an elevator pitch, even if you've never really had one. I find these to be completely boring. They remind me of those painfully awkward networking events an old manager of mine used to make me attend. Everyone was there for the sole purpose of selling you something, and business cards were being thrown down faster than your child in meltdown mode.

I teach something called a Power Pitch. Doesn't it just sound better?

Your Power Pitch is an intriguing one-sentence descriptor of who you help and what you help them with. For example: "My name is Lauren Golden, and I help moms prepare to leave their jobs to work from home on their own terms and to live a totally awesome, guilt-free life." Curious? I hope so, because if you're reading this, you are probably my ideal client.

Let's look at a few more: "I support busy entrepreneurs with tasks they don't have time to do so they can focus on scaling their business." "I equip business coaches with engaging content that converts." "I help authors expand their reach online and connect with their readers."

Once you've got a Power Pitch you can work with (don't worry, it can and will likely evolve), become a member of about five relevant Facebook or LinkedIn groups and start contributing. Answer questions and participate. Better yet, be proactive and offer value and share entertaining, informative, or helpful content (we call this storytelling). Members will start recognizing you as an expert pretty soon, no matter how green you feel.

And when someone says they're looking for help, be the person who stands out. Spend a few minutes checking out their website, their branding, and their message so that when you contact them, you can speak specifically to their needs. By doing this, you'll be ahead of 95 percent of the others who merely replied "Me!" in a Facebook thread.

Just a reminder: you need to start doing this even when you're not 100 percent sure of the next thing you'll be doing. You need to put yourself out there even when it's far from perfect.

My program provides a lot more information on how to attract clients online and in real life, but I do want to reiterate one more thing: I'm not a fan of the freelancing platforms like Upwork because they usually pay really low, have a lot of scams, and are one-off jobs.

I understand that sometimes you need to find something really fast and these can be appealing, but if it's possible to avoid them, I encourage you to market (not sell), network, and grow your business with quality clients who need repeat business.

Become an Invaluable Team Member

I could write an entire book on how to find, land, and manage your ideal client. Maybe someday I will! In the meantime, I have dozens of videos on this very topic available for free inside the Free Mama Movement Facebook group. You can also check out my *Prospect to Paid* video training and templates.

Here's what you need to know about working smarter, not harder, when it comes to finding clients. It's a heck of a lot easier to have the same clients pay you to help them over and over again than it is to constantly be out looking for new ones. Makes sense, right? I call these anchor clients, and the best-case scenario is to have them on a monthly retainer.

So how do you show up so they want to keep paying you each month? The key is to become an invaluable team member. This means giving 110 percent and wrapping up each and every project you do for them with a bow on it. Are you doing what's asked of you? Or are you over-delivering? Do you offer additional strategies, support, or solutions when appropriate? Do you take the time to truly embrace their brand and mission?

I'm not saying you shouldn't be compensated fairly for all of this amazingness. In fact, if you become invaluable, your client probably won't bat an eyelash at your rate. You're worth every penny.

One word of caution: don't overpromise if you won't be able to perform. And remember all of that talk about boundaries, expectations, and communication? It all applies here, too.

What You're NOT Going to Do

I hate to disappoint you, but here are a couple of things you will not be doing to make money: blogging, creating a logo, and working on your website.

You make money when you're working for clients in your business, not when you're working *on* your business.

I'm not saying blogs and branding aren't important. I'm saying please don't focus your attention here at the beginning. And if you choose to name your business and create a logo and build a website, please, oh, please don't get stuck here.

It will *feel* like you're working on your business, but you simply won't find freelancing clients by doing these things. At the end of the day, it just doesn't matter much.

Especially that website. Don't worry about it. Maybe you'll build one; maybe you won't. Maybe when you get past your haves and needs, you will need a kick-butt website with opt-in pages and email marketing to scale to the business you always wanted. That's amazing, and if that's where you're heading, it will be important. *Eventually*.

But you don't have to have one right now, and if you do create one, you definitely don't need to spend a bunch of time and money on it.

You're a Mama, which means you're responsible for a minimum of two humans. You may be working a full-time job. You may have twelve kids and twelve acres and a spouse. You've got plenty of other things to do with your time, so when it comes to your business, I want you to focus on income-producing activities, and all of this stuff is not that.

A Brief Word about Taxes

You're starting a freelancing business to make money, no doubt. So before you get paid on that first invoice, I want to make sure one point is crystal clear: not all of the money you receive is *actually* yours.

First, a disclaimer: I'm not a tax professional. You should consult with your CPA or accountant about your specific situation because everyone's business is different, tax laws are extremely complicated, and each state is different.

There are some general rules of thumb I can provide, however, and the first is to keep business and personal expenses separate as much as possible. Even if you operate as sole proprietor, you can open a separate checking account that only handles business expenses. If you form an LLC or some other entity, you'll have an account for that.

The IRS doesn't like any confusion on this or what it calls "comingling of funds," so the sooner you can separate it, the better. It will also make life easier on you when you file your taxes because you can easily grab the information and won't spend time separating things out throughout the year or every spring when you file.

You also may need to pay taxes quarterly. Again, consult with a professional about your specific business, but do understand that regardless of when and how often you pay it, you *will* have to set aside a portion of your profits to send to Uncle Sam. No more employer to do it on your behalf.

It's not fun to pay taxes, but remind yourself that it also means you're making money! Plus, you were *always* paying taxes. With a job you just never saw those funds first. It's also a good idea to keep taxes in mind anytime you invoice a client; *never* think of the full amount as your take-home figure and you'll save yourself a lot of heartache.

CHAPTER 16

How to Manage Your Clients Like a Boss

It's time, Mama. You've laid your plans, you've networked, you've shown people the value you have to offer, and even sent your good vibes out into the universe and then . . . someone wants to chat with you about your services.

You jump on a discovery call, and you land your first client.

It'll happen, and it may happen sooner than you think.

You da boss.

The question is, can you manage your clients like one?

This is *so* important, Mama Boss! And I want to bring you into the world of organization and flow, a place where you not only do more in less time but you know *exactly* what the "more" is and *exactly* how much time it took you.

You're going to systematize. Have I mentioned this already? (A few dozen times, perhaps?) Have I mentioned how sexy it is?

This is only the most important part of managing clients. If you don't stay on top of things, you can quickly spiral into disorganization and chaos, especially as you take on more of them, and that's no fun. More than that, it's not profitable. We set out on this journey to give you more time with your family and more joy in your life, and I'll be darned if that's going to be snatched away from you because of a lack of organization. (Whoa—strong language, I know.)

And, because I seem to like the number five, here are five questions to ask yourself before handling client work:

1. Do I know my peak time to work?

This goes beyond morning person or night owl; in fact, you may not have a choice here.

You need to figure out when you have the least amount of distractions and schedule your work accordingly. Dive even deeper and determine the level of distraction, then match the style and complexity of the task to the level.

For example, it's easy to conclude you will get nothing done when trying to shove everyone out the door for school in the morning. Don't even try. It's just not worth it, and you'll probably screw it up. Focus instead on making sure everyone brushed their teeth and isn't wearing the same thing as yesterday. Unless you washed it.

But if all of your kids are at school or day care for a blissfully quiet three hours in the morning, bingo—that's prime time. This is when you work on those things you need your full brain and attention for.

In my business, I'll work on client calls, shoot videos, do Facebook Lives, and my writing during these quiet hours. For me, this comes in the late morning; it may be different for you.

I'll work on the more technical aspects of my business in the afternoon, if I have time, or even after the kids are in bed: Clickfunnels, calendar management, and social media posting and commenting. These don't have the same sense of urgency and are also things I can work on even if there's a little more action in the house or my husband is watching a show in the background.

Figure out your peak work time and then prioritize; use it in conjunction with your Daily 5 to really kick some butt and systematize like the sexy boss Mama you are.

2. Have I eliminated any distractions?

Just because you've shoved, er, lovingly sent your angel children out the door does not mean all distractions have been eliminated.

You know where I'm going with this, don't you?

It's okay. We all have our guilty pleasures. But unless you're getting paid for them—in which case, please make sure it's legal—it's time to shut them down. Turn off the

Facebook notifications. Seriously. In fact, if you're on your phone, turn off all social media and email notifications right now. Unfollow, or even leave, 98 percent of the groups you're in. If you need a quick fix, use it as a reward. When I finish this project, I get to mindlessly scroll through Instagram for five glorious minutes.

If TV is your distraction, find a way to make it disappear. Not the flat screen but maybe the remote. Maybe the Netflix subscription. It's only temporary.

No. Freakin. Distractions. Boss time.

Still not convinced? Consider this: I promise you that you'll work twice as long and it will feel twice as hard if you let those seemingly small distractions creep in.

3. Have I prioritized what needs to be done first?

Back to the Daily 5. Once you start working with clients, their priorities become your priorities, so it's vital you communicate with them to be clear about what specifically needs to be done and by when. These are called expectations, and along with communication and boundaries (can't get enough of those), it should be one of *the* guiding principles of your new freelancing business.

Don't rely on your clients to spell this out for you; some may—if they're crazy organized like me. But a lot of others are simply looking for a lighter workload no matter how it happens, and it'll be your job to sort through and ask questions and make suggestions and figure out the order in which things get done.

By ensuring you're clear on your client's expectations, you'll be able to deliver top-notch services that keep them happily paying you month after month.

4. Do I have everything I need to complete the task?

Before you start, you need two things: to know whether you need any additional feedback from your client and to make sure you've got everything open and available before you begin.

I'll be the first to admit this one takes some experience, which means you're going to have to learn it by living it—no shortcuts.

But it won't take long. You'll soon figure out that in order to post on your client's social media accounts, you will need to know a few things about their product and how many times a day to post, not to mention the actual credentials for posting on their behalf.

I don't know a single freelancer who doesn't consistently have between ten and ten thousand tabs open. Now, if that's a distraction, get out of there. However, I frequently sit down and begin a project by opening all the tabs I'll need open to complete the entire scope of a project before I start working. This may sound like a small thing, but it disrupts your train of thought and your "flow" when you need to search for any information. Have it open to begin with and then zip through the job.

When starting client work, you'll discover it's not efficient to bounce from computer screen to desk to phone to file cabinet or attempt a bunch of back-and-forth with your client when you should instead be focused on the job at hand. Get everything organized beforehand. Do you have the log-ins or credentials you need? Do you understand exactly what to do?

Remember, your clients hardly expect you to know everything, especially everything about their business, so don't be shy about asking them for a training video if they were previously doing the task themselves. They can hop on Zoom, my favorite video-conferencing software, and walk you through the steps, which you can then turn into a manual for yourself and for them.

At the same time, don't pester your client with a bunch of questions you could find with a little resourcefulness, like heading to Google, a help desk, or even a Facebook community. Don't be lazy, but don't struggle either.

5. Am I Ready to Adapt?

Like they say in parenting: spit-up happens.

It's the same in your business. You can have your day planned perfectly and you are flying through tasks, totally in flow . . . and your client calls with an emergency, or worse, a total change in direction. Suddenly you have a new priority for your day.

Are you the type who's going to let that throw you off for the next few hours, or can you pivot? (Did you read that with Ross's voice from *Friends*? I did.) We often think that super planners (like myself) will get totally ticked off and be off-balance the rest of the day, but the opposite is actually true. When you keep on top of your schedule, focus, and organize, you are much better equipped to handle surprises.

Track Everything

Confession of a virtual hoarder: I save every email.

Every. Email. Unless I'm absolutely, positively sure I'll never need it again, that sucker gets saved.

I know, I know. In an era when Inbox Zero is the ultimate goal, you might've suspected I trash each email immediately after reading it. At least after *completing* it.

Nope. But I *do* move them into highly organized folders and systems. Why? Because you can step in and very quickly figure out where everything is.

The fact that I save every email *doesn't* mean my inbox is outrageous. I'm just a stickler for record-keeping—and you should be too! The way you set up your home, your office, and even your laptop so you know exactly where everything is, is the same approach you take with your email and files. And your clients' email and files.

I want to know where correspondence on any topic is, and I also like to keep paper trails. This doesn't mean I expect things to go poorly, but it's always a good idea to keep records. You can quickly reference previous conversations if there's ever a question about what was said. And sooner or later, we all run into miscommunications. Having a record helps you clear it up quickly and move on, which is always good for your working relationships.

And as I explained earlier, you always want to think about ways to delegate. So if you're handling client emails or record-keeping, for example, and you have a clear and organized system for doing so, someone else can easily step in and take over—leaving you available to work on something else (preferably something higher paying!).

When you're crystal clear about your record-keeping, you can also supply your clients with detailed feedback on the value you're providing them. The great thing about solving problems for other people is that you are doing something incredibly important by taking their minds off certain tasks.

The bad thing? Their minds are off certain tasks, which sometimes means they forget what a pain those were or how time-consuming. Toggl is a great app for time tracking, by the way. Not only could you provide a gentle reminder to your client with it, it's also an incentive for them to continue paying you.

Good record-keeping also means you can track what's going on with their social media, assuming you're going to help them with social media. You'll have data to report.

You can track repetitive client work activities, so if your client is asking you to track the same things over and over, you can start a Google spreadsheet for it. You can track all potential client communication, network events, speaking engagements, and inventory, then put that info into spreadsheets, too.

And, of course, you'll want to track your own income and expenses. I like QuickBooks Self-Employed, but you can easily start with an Excel spreadsheet. The important thing is to keep track of your business expenses—anything from a laptop to printer paper to professional development; yes, even the Free Mama Movement is a write-off—and remember to keep your business and personal expenses separate.

When you're a whiz at tracking, you're also able to spot minor issues before they become major problems. If a client's customer is upset about something, you can document the conversation and let your client know how well you handled it. There's nothing worse than a he said/she said in any disagreement.

And finally, you'll also be able to tell whether you've met your own goals.

Ever keep a potty chart for your toddler? Well, what about you? No, not for *that*—for your goals! Good record-keeping is like the best-ever potty chart, where, instead, your gold stars are milestones and you reward yourself with . . . well, with whatever you want!

And yes, I just compared goal-tracking to a potty chart.

CHAPTER 17

How to Quit Your Job

Remember Michael, the mentor I went to lunch with? At The Mixx in Kansas City? He also helped me plan my quitting day at work.

Technically, he helped me to *stop* planning it. I was driving myself crazy.

I was trying to role-play the whole thing—what I would say, what they might say, then what I would reply, and on and on. I was attempting to anticipate every possible scenario. What if they said this? What if they said that?

Then Michael stepped in.

"Lauren," he said, "there are literally a million ways they could react."

This was a little unnerving but also reassuring. He was right. I couldn't possibly practice and rehearse every single scenario; that was a huge waste of time. I had absolutely no control over their reaction. The only thing I could control was myself. So instead of worrying, with his help, I was able to outline my key points for the conversation.

Michael's biggest concern, which was valid even though I probably didn't want to admit it, was that I could absolutely not go in there and cry. I needed to remain as professional as possible. Heads-up—I'm a crier.

He knew how *passionate* I could sometimes be when I involved myself deeply in something, and, as sophisticated as I may have believed myself to be, I was still a late-twenty-something.

Michael did a great job at giving me a pep talk and letting me know I could do it and that it was going to be fine. He helped me prep what I would say and told me to be calm, concise, and not emotional.

And I did it. And it was not at all the awful scene I had feared, complete with a security escort out of the building. In fact, I was told how valued I was, and I turned them into my highest-paying anchor client during that same meeting!

The point is, I realize how big a deal it is to quit your job. I was in a decent position to be able to quit my job, but I was procrastinating. I was overplanning and letting fear get in the way.

Quitting is a combination of mindset and preparation, and you need to handle both. That's what we'll discuss in this chapter.

Understanding Stability

We talked about this earlier, but it's important to revisit: stability is a state of mind.

I know that's a really tough one for some of you to swallow. So many people feel like their jobs are their security, and they get lulled by the paychecks that show up week in and week out, no matter what.

You can create that same kind of consistency in a freelancing business, Mama!

Stability comes from consistently taking action, establishing a routine, living within your means, making good decisions, surrounding yourself with good people, and always growing personally and professionally.

My husband has been laid off, and I've dealt with multiple furloughs. You see companies closing all the time, even in network marketing. I've had friends who climbed the ranks in MLMs only to have the business suddenly close.

It's an illusion to think that any career is totally safe and secure.

I'm not trying to scare you, but the sooner you can appreciate that idea, the less dependent you'll feel on your employer.

Even if you're a stay-at-home mom or have already left your job, this applies to you. We're going to talk about being consistent, taking strategic action, and making over your mindset, which you'll soon learn is about 95 percent of the self-employment game.

Your Resignation Roadmap

The first thing you need to do, even before thinking about money or health insurance, is to think about who's on your team. Who will help support you? I don't just mean financially, but who will cheer you on, and help with childcare and with whatever it is you need in this journey?

I like to say it takes a village to support a Mama. Who's in your village? A spouse, other family members, friends? Make a list. If you honestly can't think of anyone, do whatever you need to do to find some sort of support group. You can start by joining the Free Mama Movement Facebook group, where we have thousands of women ready to answer questions and to lift you up.

While you're thinking about your village, also look at your timeline. *When* do you want to quit your job, and how much of your income do you absolutely have to replace before you can turn in your notice? Once you have an end date, you can work backward and fill in your plan of action.

Unless you have a nice little nest egg or do not rely on your income, you have two primary things to work on before you quit: landing at least one anchor client and keeping an eye on your pipeline.

Anchor Clients

An anchor client is a client on a monthly retainer or a longer-term contract instead of jobs that are one-off projects or done for hourly pay. You provide consistent work, and they are a regular source of income. This type of client is what provides you with a sense of security. This is the kind of client you actually want to work with for the long haul.

With an anchor client, you'll have a continual flow of cash while you work to land other contracts and establish yourself. You may sign a six-month or even a one-year contract, and you may need to offer incentives to make it happen, like 10 percent off your packages if they'll sign a one-year contract. You'll probably bill monthly, though it could be more often depending on your proposal and what you both agree to. Communication. Expectations. Together with your client, you get to decide these things!

I want you to focus on landing at least one high-paying anchor client before you leave your job if your family relies on your income. At the same time, keep in mind that you'll still be looking for others and may very well still need to take a few one-off jobs. Remember how traditional employment is the ultimate eggs-in-one-basket scenario? It's important to stay diversified. Businesses change direction all the time, and that anchor client may not need your services anymore when your contract is up.

Your Pipeline

Don't wait until you've lost one client to look for another one!

Even if your work with your anchor client keeps your schedule packed, make sure to find time to meet new, prospective clients and consider other work. Always keep an eye on the end of the contract—you'll know when it's coming since you're tracking everything so well now—so that you can avoid the cash droughts.

You should continually update your website with testimonials and the new services you have in place. Keep your LinkedIn profile updated. Ask your clients for repeat business, called renewals, and referrals. Business owners tend to know other business owners.

Even when you feel like you've reached your capacity in your freelancing business, you should always be like Ray the farmer—planting seeds.

Plan for Your Must-Haves

Earlier, we talked about wants, needs, and haves. And I've emphasized that you'll have to get those haves taken care of before anything else.

So before you quit your job, get really detailed about those haves. This information will guide your plan.

How much money do you need to pay your monthly bills? What's that exact number? Do you need to add health-insurance costs, or will you have insurance through your spouse?

There are lots of apps available to help you track your money and to budget so you know exactly what's going on with it. This is hugely important, Mama.

I understand it's also scary and uncomfortable and is one of those things you totally don't want to deal with. But this isn't like peas on your dinner plate. You can't sneak this to the dog when nobody's looking.

You're a grown-up now, and part of adulting is that we take control of our finances and our insurance and figure it out. Sure, it sucks. But it's the only path available if you want to quit your job. Think of it like choking down your vegetables to get to dessert. Totally worth it in the end.

Whatever Is Holding You Back

We've talked about a lot so far. And it can get overwhelming, I know.

I see a lot of Mamas whose eyes glaze over at this point, kind of like the way my kids look at me when I tell them to put on their shoes *and* brush their teeth. It feels like too much.

If you're nervous, there are probably a few things going on. The first is that this is all new, and we've covered a lot of material, and you're facing the unknown. That one's pretty easy to deal with: just slow things down and focus on each step as you go. Take little steps and keep moving forward. Start with one phone call to a health-insurance rep. That's it for today. One step at a time.

Of course, there is the money concern. It is totally valid. A girl's gotta eat! But it's just a numbers game. It's math. You can sort that stuff out.

Another issue could be that you've never hung around with people who do this kind of thing. And maybe your current clique is not very encouraging.

More tough love, Mama: life only comes around once. Spend it doing what makes you feel happy, fulfilled, and free.

I'm guessing your soul-sucking job and equally miserable coworkers aren't cutting it in the personal-development space.

It's said you are the average of the five people you spend the most time with. Who are they? Do they lift you up and want the best for you? If not, maybe it's time to reevaluate who you're hanging out with.

I get it—sometimes the negativity is within your immediate family and there's not much you can do to get away from it. But other times, we're simply spending time with people who sap our energy. Misery loves company.

It can be really uncomfortable to pull away from that, but if you're serious about becoming a Free Mama, this may be one of those difficult steps you need to take in order to set yourself free. It's important to build a support system, whether that means joining my Facebook group, where other Mamas will root for you, or whether you can physically spend more time around positive, uplifting, successful people.

Also pay attention to what *you're* focusing on. Are you putting your time and energy into things that lift you up and inspire you, or are you focused on all the things that are difficult?

Sometimes we don't even notice it; it's amazing how often we'll phrase things in the negative. We can tell our kids not to stand on the table, for example, or we can tell them to sit in their chair. It's the same message but approached from different angles. And if you're my daughter, you often hear it both ways. I'm working on it.

There are a few other reasons people stay stuck: lack of clarity, a feeling they don't have the ability, or lack of motivation.

Often, you'll solve the clarity issue with action—just start doing *something*, and it will help you sort through the details and to zero in on a plan you enjoy. Or maybe you need to reach out to your support system and talk through it a little more so you can figure out those first steps.

Action also helps when you don't know whether you've got the ability. You'll surprise yourself with how much you know when you actually get out there and start doing. You know more than you think you do, I promise.

As for motivation? This one's on you. This goes back to finding your why and keeping it in front of you at all times. I don't care if you have to print it out and stick it to your bathroom mirror and your steering wheel. Get that why all up in your face.

And finally, Mama, I give you an out: you can always go back to a job.

Gasp.

Listen, if a safety net is what you need, a safety net is what you'll get. You won't need it, but if that's what it takes to make you relax, you got it!

Let's end this chapter with a little woo woo. Have you ever heard of manifesting? I want you to manifest a kick-butt life for yourself, Mama.

Close your eyes and focus on what you want and make it look real. Your brain can't tell the difference, so feed it something awesome. What will it look like when you finally get to quit your job and can have breakfast as a family? When you can stay home with your kids? When you create financial stability for yourself?

Do this exercise for real, and feel the feels. Make it look real in your mind.

You can have all that. I know you can, and I believe in you.

CHAPTER 18

How to Believe in Yourself

Can you believe how much we've covered in this book? You now know what it means to have it all and that *you* are your biggest asset when it comes to making that happen.

You have strategies to help you with time management, setting boundaries, and maneuvering through difficult decisions. You've defined your why, established a few SMART goals, set up sexy systems, prioritized, gotten tools to become more polished and professional, and laid out a business plan.

It's go time, Mama.

It's time to stop reading and thinking and studying. Time to stop watching every free webinar that pops up on your news feed. It's time to put this book down and get out in the real world already. I mean, once you've finished this chapter.

How does that make you feel? I hope you're excited! I know it may also freak you out a little bit. That's totally normal. It means you're growing.

Remember, the most important thing isn't the tools or the strategy. The most important part is whether you *believe* you can do this. Whether you think you can or think you cannot, you're right.

Tough-love gut check: if your first thought is that you can't do this, you're toast.

Does that mean you don't still have one hundred more questions for me that didn't fit into this book? Or that you don't have fear or doubt or that you won't sometimes feel a little lost? You will totally feel all those things, often at the same time.

But do you *believe you can do it anyway*?

That Time Self-Doubt Voted in My Place

I've always been a pretty confident person, but let me tell you a story about a time when self-doubt got the better of me. This one's from high school again, where most of our super-awesome stories about insecurity stem from. Besides, I couldn't finish this book without one more dance reference.

My freshman year of dance team, I was so scared to go to the state competition. That's as big as it gets, and our team was so good—and what if *I* screwed it up and was the reason the team didn't win? What if everyone hated me?

And I got kicked off the team? Everything seemed so big and so scary to this little freshman on the varsity team.

And then it got even *scarier* my sophomore year.

We had the opportunity to travel to Orlando, Florida, and compete in the United Dance Association's National Championship. NATIONALS. It would be a huge commitment with more practices and routines, and we'd have to fund-raise our way there. Our coach set up an anonymous vote on whether we'd go. She knew she couldn't make us do it, that we had to want it for ourselves.

Mama, I was beyond scared. I was terrified. It sounded so much bigger than I was, it was totally unfamiliar, and I knew our coach was going to kick our butts with a personal trainer and everything else that goes into prepping for something at that level. I sat on the bleachers in that old, non-air-conditioned gym, and my heart started beating out of my chest with anxiety just thinking about the whole thing.

I voted no.

That's kind of embarrassing to admit, and I'm pretty sure until now I've only told like three people, but I'll confess: I voted no because I led with fear. All I could picture was everything that might go wrong instead of the unbelievable opportunity in front of me. I couldn't see past my fear.

Thankfully, the team voted yes. And, long story short, we went to nationals and placed in the top ten two out of three years.

It was terrifying, but it was also incredibly rewarding. To this day, it remains one of my biggest accomplishments. It was super hard, but it was worth it.

It was a big, huge, crazy-scary goal—and my team went for it.

I'm so grateful the team voted yes, because it taught me so many lessons. And it started a pattern. If we had passed on the chance, we would have given ourselves permission to duck out of something epic just because we were afraid of it. And when you do that once, it gets easier to do it again.

The irony is that it works both ways: it gets easier to hold yourself back, but it also gets easier to do something brave. So the choice is yours. You can start a pattern of hiding, or one of taking on challenges.

That moment in the gym didn't become a big deal until we actually went and I realized I had made the wrong choice when I voted no months earlier. I realized I had been operating out of fear.

It took awhile for the lesson to sink in. I was nervous for a long time leading up to the competition, and only then, when I experienced it in person, did I start to think maybe I was qualified to be there with all those other dancers. It wasn't until we got to Orlando that the whole thing got out of my head and into real life. And once I was there and doing it, my nerves were manageable. I was more excited than afraid.

I realized there's a simple formula for believing in yourself.

Decision + Action + Experience = Empowerment

Say yes, do something, do it again, and you'll begin to become more confident. That's the way it works.

We went back to nationals my junior and senior years. Each time, it got way easier. I was still nervous to perform, but I felt stronger and more confident.

From Overwhelmed to Empowered

There's only one way to succeed, Mama, and that's with action. Walk the walk.

Whether it's the high kick, high tech, or self-employment, success involves the same journey of moving from overwhelmed to empowered. And action is what motors you and makes the whole journey happen.

I get it: You don't like doing things you aren't naturally good at. You think maybe you'll buy a few more courses and read a few more books until you figure it out and you'll start somewhere in the middle. You'll be ahead of the curve.

But in business, *nobody* gets to start in the middle (bummer, I know). You need to start doing something, right here, right now, imperfections and all. You need to be a beginner for just a little while.

And don't forget, you've done this before! Never overlook the lessons that being a mother has taught you, and never forget that being a mom is one of the fiercest things you've ever done.

You certainly didn't start in the middle with motherhood. I know you were scared and overwhelmed and filled with self-doubt, and maybe even a little clueless (we all were). I also know you took the childbirth class and read the books and that none of it helped. But your precious baby came into this world, and then you figured it out. You kept on learning.

I don't care what kind of plan you had, you started out having no idea what you were doing. Then you had one small win after another. The baby latched on. Slept through the night. Remembered to flush the toilet. Shared her toys with a friend. Got up for school by himself.

And you gained confidence!

You didn't start motherhood by handing out life wisdom to your high school graduate as she departed for college. You started out changing a diaper and calming a crying baby.

Same thing here.

Come from a place of service in your freelancing business. Solve a problem for someone. Get paid. It can be checking their email, for goodness sake. You don't have to know it all, and you don't have to have everything figured out just yet.

Whenever I've felt overwhelm, it's usually because I'm trying to do too much at once or when I skip ahead. I'm thinking about college-level advice when I should be thinking about dealing with a newborn.

And I *still* feel overwhelmed sometimes, Mama. It's just at a different level now. I went through it as I finished writing this book, until my coach helped me pick a few areas to focus on while setting the rest of my big plans aside for the moment. The *Today Show* will have to wait.

Self-employment is the greatest personal-development course you'll ever take. I have watched so many women start in a place of fear and overwhelm and self-doubt only to take action and push through it. They are now more *confident* than ever, and they just thought they were signing up to make money from home.

I want that for you.

And the Free Mama Movement is here for you.

To point you in the right direction.

To provide the roadmap and framework.

What I cannot do is the work for you. No one can. That part—taking action and stepping through your fear and uncertainty—you must do on your own.

Decision + Action + Experience = Empowerment

Decide you're going to do this and start doing it. What you focus on expands, so find small wins in everything you do, and you'll soon see more of them.

I don't care what action you take, just do something. Mama, I felt overwhelmed at the thought of writing a book! But now that I'm in this final chapter and it's almost done, I feel empowered. It didn't happen overnight. Most of the time I had absolutely no clue what I was doing. But I surrounded myself with others who had done it, and when I got stuck, I invested in people who could help me.

This book is something I've thought about doing for a long time. My deepest sense of personal success, however, comes from the fact that I did it, and that all started with a decision. Whether it's a book, or a business, or landing that first client, or finally telling your mom what you're up to, or having your children be proud of you, empowerment comes from the doing. Not the thinking about doing.

I believe in you, and I hope by now you believe in yourself. Whether you think you can or think you cannot, you're right.

So get out there, Mama. You've got this. I know you can do it!

Conclusion

WHAT'S NEXT?

Wow! Here we are at the end of this book.

I hope your wheels are turning, Mama. I hope that something in you has been ignited (or reignited, as the case may be). And I also hope that you feel equipped with the tools to actually go out and do whatever it is that you're noodling right now.

Not just *start* it...

But consistently, day after day, one intentional action after another, even on the days you're fearful and riddled with doubt or slapped with rejection, *do* the darn thing.

You *will* do it imperfectly.

But you will be *doing* it. And you will get better. And better yet.

Like I mentioned at the beginning of this book, life is full of choices. Only you get to choose what you do after you set this book down.

You decide what comes next.

If you're ready to keep going, and you don't want to do it alone, I have great news! The Free Mama is so much more than the words you've read here. It's a community of thousands of women who feel just like you do and are ready to support, encourage and teach you. It's resources, programs and mentorship to help you get better quicker, many of which can be found below.

And it's you.

You are now officially a Free Mama.

Resource #1: The Free Mama Community

How would you feel if you could be friends with thousands of mamas who play nicely and lift each other up? This community exists - and it's free! There are 3 ground rules: be kind, be supportive, take action. That's it! If you can do that, you're invited to join us:

www.facebook.com/groups/thefreemamamovement

Resource #2: The Daily 5

Do you start each morning anxious about all of the things on your plate?

What if there was a way to quickly and effectively write your to-do list that was limited to the action-items that will get you closer towards achieving your goals?

Enter the last productivity planner you'll ever need. Download your *free* planner and learn more about the The Daily 5:

https://thefreemama.com/thedaily5

Resource #3: The Free Mama Webinar

Would you like the freedom to work from home and spend more time with your family? Do you want to know how to start a business doing simple administrative and marketing tasks for entrepreneurs who are starving for your help?

In this free training I'm going to show you my specific method for freelancing from home that allows me to have a ton of fun doing things I enjoy, make the maximum amount of money for the time I put in, and spend more time with my family. You'll learn how I became a highly paid virtual administrative consultant, and how I've taught over 600 other moms how to do it, too.

www.thefreemamamovement.com

Resource #4: The Free Mama Movement

Are you ready to join The Free Mama Movement?

Replace your income from home as a Virtual Administrative Consultant in just three months! My 12-week program teaches you how to start your new freelance business and replace your 9-5 salary — with plenty of hands-on support and step-by-step guidance.

www.thefreemamamovement.com/go

Resource #5: Quick Start Freelance Success Kit

If you can read the words on this page, you can do the work necessary to start your own business, scale up or down according to what works best for you and your family, and earn the money that will let you stay home with your kids.

You're nervous about this freelancing thing, and that makes sense. This 3-module course will give you the information you need to assess your existing skills and figure out exactly how you can earn money freelancing from home.

https://www.thefreemamamovement.com/success

About the Author

Lauren Golden loves helping mamas free themselves from the 9-5 grind. She launched The Free Mama Movement to show working moms that they don't have to choose between family and financial stability.

Hundreds of families today are happier and more fulfilled thanks to Lauren and her online programs. Whether you're a single mom, a military mom, or a mom in a two-parent family who doesn't want to sacrifice your time with your babies in order to provide for them, Lauren wants you to know that you don't have to.

Today, as the fearless leader of The Free Mama Movement and a thriving community of tens of thousands of women, Lauren is passionate about showing other moms how to start and run a successful freelancing business from home. In her upcoming book, she shares her own story — along with plenty of practical advice for anyone looking to leave the 9-5 behind and make a real living from home.

In addition to her self-paced program, Lauren also works one-on-one with motivated mamas who want to get their businesses up and running fast. Her talks on freelancing, building a business, and making over your mindset, and other relevant topics resonate with women around the world.

Lauren also runs The Free Mama Matchmaker Service, where she connects graduates of her elite online program with entrepreneurs who need their specialized skills.

Learn more at TheFreeMama.com.

CPSIA information can be obtained
at www.ICGtesting.com
Printed in the USA
BVHW082249300919
559810BV00009B/508/P